The Universal Laws
and
Jesus' Meaning of
The Beatitudes

Channeled from the Spiritual Hierarchy and
The Master Jesus to

bj King

1st WORLD
PUBLISHING

The Universal Laws and
Jesus' Meaning of The Beatitudes
bj King

Copyright © 2025 by bj King

Published by 1st World Publishing
P.O. Box 2211, Fairfield, Iowa 52556
tel: 641-209-5000 • fax: 866-440-5234
web: www.1stworldpublishing.com

First Edition

ISBN Softcover: 978-1-4218-3586-0

LCCN: Library of Congress Cataloging-in-Publication Data

Table of Contents

1.

Introduction by bj King

Our Universe is perfectly balanced by natural and spiritual Laws. These Laws maintain an order we have a tendency to take for granted. We can consciously learn these Laws. If we learn these Laws, we can also learn to live in alignment with them and have order in our lives. We live on a dualistic and physical planet. Because of this, we often find ourselves faced with seeming paradoxes, caught in an endless loop of contradictions. However, it is important to remember, what we sow in consciousness, we reap. If we turn on a tape recorder and record our voice, when we play it back, what we hear will be our own voice saying exactly what we said. If we plant a spinach seed, spinach will grow, not a cauliflower. The same is true with our words and thoughts. What we think and say becomes our reality. We can depend on these Laws and use them, or we can remain ignorant and confused and pretend our life is happening to us randomly. We can only <u>pretend</u> not to be in control.

Scientists have worked to prove the laws of physics, the laws affecting our physical Universe, without considering spiritual Law or the fact that we are a self-evolving species; our thoughts control our lives and our evolution. They work to convince us we live in a World where everything takes place in relationship to deterministic laws that unfold in linear time and are unresponsive to Human thoughts or affairs. Scientists, until they developed the chaos theory, have said that chance events only produce patterns that are random, and to see meaning in such patterns is as pointless as looking for messages in the interference we call "snow" which, at certain times, appears on a television screen. To believe certain chance events are a manifestation of some underlying pattern of Nature, or are the result of "a causal connecting principle," would be utter nonsense to most scientists.

Scientists are, however, beginning to suspect even chaos has a pattern. Despite our appeal to a "scientific" view of nature, such chance or synchronistic events do occur, and while it is true any of them can be dismissed as "coincidence," such an explanation makes little sense to those of us who have experienced synchronicity. These events are meaningful and play a significant role in our lives. Usually, it is easier to see them when we look back on our lives, rather than when they are happening. It is a part of spiritual maturity to begin to recognize them while they are happening and to learn to build on them and to actually invite them into our lives.

My own personal theory is that these events are synchronized or "set up" by our Oversouls, or by "the hand of God", if you will. The Oversoul arranges certain surprise encounters or events in order to surprise us into a lesson, to assist us with our goal or, sometimes, simply for the purpose of cosmic humor. These events, however, are aligned with some thought, goal or desire we have been holding in our conscious or subconscious mind.

"Seriality" is another interesting word which is defined as "a lawful recurrence, or clustering, in time and space, whereby individual members of the sequence – as far as can be ascertained by careful analysis – are not connected by the same active source. "Serialist" events seem to take place under the influence of causal connections rather than by means of the familiar causal pushes and pulls of physics. Therefore, these events produce an argument for the existence of an underlying harmony or mosaic to nature, which includes Human thoughts and feelings affecting science or scientific experiments. What truly differentiates a synchronicity from a mere coincidence is the inherent meaning that is given to the event by us. Universal Laws do not change, but their effect can be changed by Human thought.

We are each a result of a balance between intuition, thinking, feeling and sensation. The more of our past karma and fears we release from our bodies and our subconscious, the more space we have within us for these functions to take place. Without the debris or garbage of the past, we can become systems that function in synchronicity with nature and Universal Laws. If we add to that a conscious awareness that we receive intuitive impulses, or messages, of how to stay on track, or "in the flow," we increase the occurrences of synchronicity and serendipity in our lives.

"Serendipity" is defined as the faculty of making happy and unexpected discoveries by accident or events which happen when we begin to "dip" into life with "serenity." Webster calls it "the gift of finding valuable or agreeable things not sought for." It refers to the discovery of goals which you stumble into (or which stumble into you) while you are on a search for an altogether different goal.

Serendipity is an unexpected discovery of something worthwhile during a search for an expected something worthwhile. The challenge is to accept the unexpected, or at least to pause to analyze what these un-looked-for happenings may mean in relation to the total business of living. Like many of the finest things of life, such as happiness, tranquility and fame, the gain that is most precious is not the thing sought, but one that comes of itself in the search for something else. Such are many scientific breakthroughs like sticky notes, the nicotine patch, the hormone patch, pain patches, Velcro and penicillin.

Spiritual Laws are vibrations set into place as guidelines to assist one in the selection of an efficient, satisfying and healthy path and to assist Humans in avoiding errors in the pursuit of their life. Spiritual Laws are not established to punish or to take away, but are guidelines. Each individual is responsible for their own interpretation and application of the Laws in their life. These Laws are not something to rebel against or to avoid.

2.

Introduction to Universal Laws

Channeled through bj King
From the consciousness of Matthew, previously one of Jesus' disciples

"You have often asked me to explain to you the Universal Laws. Now we are ready to begin. I will give you some of the information directly, and for some, I will give you references to other previously written information that will aid you in understanding.

"History tells you before a certain time Humankind was not aware of fire. Before a certain time, Humankind was not aware of electricity, did not understand gravity, the power of steam or the power of splitting the atom. These things have all been revealed to Humankind as they have become ready to understand and utilize these powers. It is now time that Humankind becomes aware of the power stored in a grain of sand, the power in a mustard seed, and the power of crystals. The Laws of Nature have always been the same. Only Human awareness is different. The fact most people do not suspect the existence of this Power of which I speak does not change the fact that it is there. As long as your Universe has existed, The Universal Laws have existed. The Law of Gravity worked long before it was understood by Humans and is now taken for granted by Humans. The Law which causes a planted mustard seed to produce only a mustard plant and not a rose is taken for granted without being fully understood by Humanity.

"Humanity was given the blueprint of this Power and how to utilize it through Jesus in the Sermon on the Mount. Jesus illustrated the truth about the illusion of death graphically in the crucifixion and resurrection and proved the Law of Ascension. The message was so dramatic and yet so veiled all but a few missed the true significance of the message and

the power made available to them by these events. I wrote the message as closely as I could remember it in my journal of the events of the years I spent with Jesus two thousand years ago in the embodiment of Matthew. Those who have tried to interpret it for others have tried to understand from a distorted version offered to them by those who have erroneously translated the message and the meaning. The Christian Church is based on these erroneous interpretations. You will notice I did not say the Christian Faith, but the Christian Church, which are two very different things. Those who read the Bible for themselves and pray for Divine Wisdom to enlighten them will develop the Christian Faith. Those who join, attend, and worship only through the Christian Church and their interpretations of the Bible, without reading it for their own insights, practice the Christian Church, not the Christian Faith.

"Jesus, the man, became the Christ when the Holy Spirit infused Him with the energies of the Cosmic Christ Consciousness at the time of His baptism by John the Baptist. For Him to bring this energy to Earth, while the Earth and Humanity were still so dense energetically, was a remarkable feat both for Him as a Human and as a divine being. The friendship of those of us who walked with Him was no less remarkable. We slept together, ate together, laughed and cried together and had disagreements as we tried to understand the significance of what was happening in and through us, very much as those of you who are offering to embody the Cosmic Christ Consciousness for Earth and Humanity are doing at this time. We had the same struggles you have; we had even greater opposition than you have, because His teachings were so radically opposed to that which we had been taught by the Rabbis.

"Jesus taught of the true nature of GOD, of Humanity, of life, of the World and of the relationships which exist between them. His teachings offer a practical method for the development of the soul and for the shaping of lives into joy-filled experiences, which evolve not only the soul, but also the entire species of Humanity. Jesus did not, nor did any of those of us who traveled with Him, teach theology or that churches should be created in which these teachings should be presented. Doctrines, theologies, dogmas, philosophies and churches were all the decision and creation of men and are not GOD ordained. Jesus taught Spirit and soul infusion and the illusion of death through ascension. The explanation of Humanity's life lies in the fact that they are essentially spiritual and eternal. It is exactly that which makes it possible for me to speak to you now. Death is a transition state from one level of vibration to another. It is the shedding of the physical form to retake

its original form, which is Spirit.

"Jesus' teachings have been sadly misunderstood and misrepresented. He taught that the wages of sin are high, but He did not teach of any punishment which would be other than self-inflicted, or of any judgment that would not be self-induced. He taught that GOD, His Father and ours, is an all-forgiving GOD, a loving GOD. He taught GOD would give us the strength, if we asked, to overcome any form of adversity we had, out of our ignorance, created for ourselves. He taught, we did not need to remain ignorant, but that FREE WILL, which was a gift of GOD, would not be overridden unless we prayed for assistance.

"Jesus taught principles only. He taught Holy Spirit infusion, spiritual power, spiritual comfort and assistance. He taught, there are certain LAWS which run the Universe in which we live. He did not teach the Sabbath, but taught us to make each and every day a spiritual day by constantly having spiritual attitudes and thoughts. He taught us that our thoughts created our reality. He taught us to have character and integrity. He taught us to make decisions about what we believed by watching Him and believing that it was possible for us to use these same LAWS, which He demonstrated to us, to heal our lives and to create lives filled with joy and love. He meant what He said, 'the works I do, ye shall do, and greater works'.

"Your translations of the Bible have been changed, misinterpreted and misprinted. Many of the writings have been attributed to those other than who wrote them; however, the Bible is an inspired document which contains much truth. Who wrote what and under what circumstances they wrote them is immaterial now. What is important is the spirit and intention with which it was originally written and the spirit and intention with which it is read and repeated today. <u>Divine Wisdom is the author, as it has been for many works written since then</u>. Any book can be read to gain spiritual wisdom and inspiration if that is the intention of the reader. Divine Wisdom is always available to those who ask.

"In this work you and I will attempt to explain in more detail, and with greater simplicity, the UNIVERSAL LAWS, their meanings and uses, but first let's look at the OLD LAWS."

3.

The Ten Commandments
The Old Law

Matthew continued to speak: "The OLD LAW, dealing mostly with lower states of race consciousness, concerned itself primarily with external things--for Humanity's apparent evolution is from the outer to the inner, just as his fundamental spiritual growth is from the inner to the outer. Humanity begins by giving its attention exclusively to externals, thinking to find in them cause as well as effect; but as Humans progress in evolution, the truth will gradually dawn upon Humans that outer things are but the finished article, the result of causes and happenings on the inner. When one has reached this stage, they have definitely started upon the search for GOD or FIRST CAUSE. The OLD LAW concerned itself, at least in the letter, with external observances almost completely. The LAW was satisfied when external observances were fulfilled. The Commandments said "Thou shalt not kill,' and provided a person did not murder, they kept the Law, regardless of how much they may have desired to commit murder or how bitterly they might still hate their enemy. It said "Thou shalt not steal,' and provided one did not appropriate their neighbor's property, they were held to have fulfilled the LAW, irrespective of how they felt about it.

"The OLD LAW was given to Moses. It was offered to a primitive and barbarous people who needed to be persuaded not to murder those who had offended them, to not steal from one another, to not lie, to not cheat. The OLD LAW was given to encourage Humans to master enough self-control to master their anger, their lust and desires.

"Jesus came to carry the Human race forward to the next great step, the most important step of all, which can be the next step in overcoming all

Human limitations, if Humans can understand what that step implies, and take it. The message of The Sermon on the Mount and the Lord's Prayer gives us this information. The Beatitudes were the NEW LAW given to a more highly evolved group of Humanity. The Beatitudes, when translated from Aramaic, were inaccurate in the King James Version of the Bible, according to the Master Jesus. It was time for Humans to understand outer conformity, even though essential, is no longer sufficient in itself; but now, if Humans are to come of age spiritually, they have not merely to conform outwardly to outer rules, but to change their inner selves as well. Not only are Humans admonished not to kill, steal, cheat or lie, Humans are encouraged not to think about these things or to hold anger in their bodies and minds. It is simply not possible to hold maximum amounts of the Cosmic Christ Consciousness energy vibration in a body which also holds anger, resentment, criticism, judgment, indignation or condemnation. These thoughts are as holes in a sieve, energy leaks through them, or as dregs in the bottom of a coffee cup, contaminating all that is added. A person who holds onto these negative and judgmental thoughts, or practices them, cannot hold enough energy or channel enough energy through their vehicles to exhibit <u>positive</u> or successful demonstrations of Spiritual Law.

WE MAY HAVE EITHER FEAR, ANGER, JEALOUSY OR INDIGNATION, OR POSITIVE DEMONSTRATION; NOT BOTH.

"The Universal Laws are scientific, spiritual and impersonal. Gravity affects all objects. Water seeks its own level. The angles of a triangle always add up to 180 degrees. Light travels at 186,000 miles per second. A spinach seed will yield a spinach plant. These Laws always work. They operate whether they are mentally known or understood - they operate without discrimination. Physical laws and Spiritual Laws operate in the same manner. They operate whether Humans know about them or understand them, but to understand them gives one the power to knowingly live within them and to use them for good.

"The Ten Commandments were given for a very different time, a different level of Human evolution. They were given to Moses by a being call Jehovah who then held the position of Lord of Earth. In my understanding from Spirit, the Bible is not written about the Creator God, but about a time period in history when the Earth was ruled over by two different beings, Jehovah and Yahweh, who held at different times the Spiritual Hierarchy

position of Lord of Earth."

Receiving this insight from Matthew made it possible for me to understand the dramatic difference between the God of the Old Testament and the God of the New Testament, but neither God seemed to be the God I now believe in -- the Creator God of all Universes.

THE OLD TESTAMENT

According to Dr. Frank Alper in his book, *Universal Law for the Aquarian Age*, the Ten Commandments for this Age might be rewritten as follows:

THE OLD: Jehovah said, "I am the Lord your God who brought you out of Egypt, out of the land of slavery. You shall have no other Gods before me."

THE NEW: *"I AM the Lord your God. You shall place no other want, desire, or need before Me, for I AM and I AM all that is."*

This would basically mean Humans should use caution not to place our greed, our emotional desires, our ego desires in front of our recognition of the God within. God would actually be saying "recognize I AM within you." In recognizing God within us, it is impossible to deny God's existence and impossible to not recognize that we were created to be conduits for God's energy on Earth.

THE OLD: Jehovah said, "You shall not make for yourself an idol in the form of Heaven above, or on the Earth beneath, or in the waters below. You shall not bow down to them or worship them, for I, the Lord your God, am a jealous God, punishing the children for the sins of the fathers to the third and fourth generation of those who hate me, but showing love to thousands who love Me and keep My Commandments."

THE NEW: *"I AM the Lord your God. I AM Love and Light, I AM All Seeing, All Knowing and All Benevolent, and I allow you the freedom of choice and freedom of will to take any action you wish during the course of your lives, as long as you also take responsibility for the results of your actions. If you wish to err, I bless you and charge you with the responsibility to learn from the error, but the choice is yours."*

If we look at the rewording of the Law, we find we are assuming responsibility for our actions, our thoughts, our ideas, for we have reached the point in our evolution where we are capable of handling this type of responsibility and accounting to ourselves for our actions. We know we are responsible to ourselves and our God, in Its benevolence, allows us to choose our actions no matter what.

THE OLD: Jehovah said, "You shall not misuse the Name of the Lord your God, for the Lord will not hold anyone guiltless who misuses His Name. Or thou shalt not use the Name of thy Lord in vain."

THE NEW: "*God is within you; therefore, thou shalt not take thy name in vain; thou shalt not hold thyself in ridicule; thou shalt not hold thyself in shame. I am saying the same thing. The only variation is I am holding you accountable to yourselves. I am demanding you recognize the God within.*"

This change makes us once again responsible for ourselves and our relationship to ourselves and the God within us as us.

THE OLD: Jehovah said, "Observe the Sabbath Day by keeping it Holy as the Lord your God has commanded you. Six days shall you labor and do all your work, but the evening and seventh day is a Sabbath to the Lord your God. On it you shall not do any work, neither you, nor your son or daughter, nor your manservant nor your maidservant nor your ox, nor your donkey, or any of your animals, nor the aliens within your gates, so your manservants and maidservants may rest as you do. Remember that you were slaves in Egypt and that the Lord your God brought you out of there with a mighty hand and an outstretched arm. Therefore, the Lord your God has commanded you to observe the Sabbath Day."

THE NEW: "*Labor for six days, and on the seventh, contemplate your growth, care for yourself, nurture and love yourself. Bless God for giving you the strength to put forth effort for growth during the past six days. Recharge your bodies and your minds so you may undertake a new week with vigor, strength and health.*"

To overwork our bodies and minds is a disservice to our vehicles which house the God within.

THE OLD: Jehovah said, "Honor your Father and your Mother as the Lord your God has commanded you, so you may live long, so it may go well with you in the land the Lord your God is giving you."

THE NEW: *"This could also be taken to mean honor the heavens and the Earth, care for what God has given you, respect it, recognize its existence. Give recognition, respect and acceptance to yourself and others."*

Recognize the Earth and everyone on the Earth as part of the Oneness of the Creator God.

THE OLD: Jehovah said, "Thou shalt not commit murder."

THE NEW: *The Law was not worded, "Thou shalt not cause death," for there is no death. Thou shalt not end another's cycle; thou shalt not murder another's ambition; thou shalt not murder another's desire; thou shalt not murder thy love of God."*

THE OLD: Jehovah said, "Thou shalt not commit adultery."

THE NEW: *"Thou shall have respect for others."*

If a man and a man, a woman and a woman, or a man and a woman are involved with each other in any type of relationship of an intimate nature of their own free will and desire, then they, and they alone, must assume the responsibility for their actions; if they take this action, and it is their truth at all levels of awareness, then they have committed nothing but a union. However, if living and enacting their truth causes harm or damage to another Human being, and this damage is the result of a breach of contract, then the responsibility for this damage falls upon them.

THE OLD: Jehovah said, "Thou shalt not steal."

THE NEW: *"To own things is an illusion. We are allowed the responsibility of stewardship, not ownership. To take something that is not assigned to us for stewardship, something that is another's responsibility, is against spiritual Law."*

To claim ownership of channeled information (and all information is channeled) is an illusion.

THE OLD: Jehovah said, "Thou shalt not bear false witness against thy neighbor."

THE NEW: *"Thou shalt not lead the minds of others astray by relating personal judgments against thy neighbors." Merely gossiping gives false testimony against thy neighbor. When relating your discernment to another moves from discernment to judgment, that is false witness.*

To discern is to know from the level of your soul and awareness if a thing is true for you or appropriate for you. To judge is to discern and to take the discernment further by relating it to another. Example: When you discern, another person cannot be trusted is discernment. When you discern this, then add the judgment this person cannot be trusted by anyone, and will never be trustworthy, is to judge.

THE OLD: Jehovah said, "Thou shalt not covet your neighbor's wife. Thou shalt not set your desires on your neighbor's house, or land, his servants, his animals, or anything that belongs to your neighbor."

THE NEW: *"Do not covet what is not yours, and have the faith and knowledge that the flow of life shall provide you with your needs and, if you are lucky enough, with some of your desires as well."*

If you do not desire, you do not grow. What is the difference between the words admire and desire? If you admire another man's wife, does that mean you are coveting her? If you desire her, and allow her to become aware of your feelings, then you are coveting her, for you have taken an action upon a thought. To fantasize is not to covet; many times, it is a stimulus for one to create their own fantasy and to do for themselves. To covet is to desire, but to the extent that it interferes with the normal course of life and becomes an all-consuming passion, is the error.

4.

The Universal Laws

The Universe is one of Law, order and harmony,
not a result of mere chance or accident.

Our belief or disbelief in the Law does not change the Law.

We are spiritual beings living in a spiritual Universe, governed by spiritual and physical Universal Laws; therefore, it will serve us to understand these Laws. The purpose of these laws is to maintain order in the Universe. The more we understand and rely on Universal Laws to work for us, the more we will experience perfection in our lives.

LAW OF ABUNDANCE:

The LAW OF ABUNDANCE is based on blessing, giving, receiving and accepting. We live in an abundant Universe. Abundance is our birth-right as aspects of a loving God. We are to acknowledge what we have by <u>blessing</u> it, being grateful for and caring for what we have. We are to live with <u>grateful</u> hearts. For every accomplishment and good that enters our lives, we are to consciously give thanks. By blessing <u>all</u> situations, we increase the potential for harmony and abundance to be established in our lives. We have a tendency to judge certain situations and events as positive and certain situations and events as negative. When we learn to bless all events for <u>positive content</u>, more and more positive, abundant events will be attracted into our lives. The person who uses well what they are given will receive more, but those who hoard or use improperly what they are given will lose what they have.

The Universe works for and with us. It is not our enemy.

Take a stand for what you desire, rather than battle with what you say you don't desire. You wouldn't go to a cafeteria and tell the person behind the counter all the things you don't desire to eat. You would not order something from a catalog without stating the size and color you desire. Be specific about your desires. Do not use the words "want" and "need." Your subconscious and your soul take you literally and think you desire to continue to want or continue to need, rather than to receive. It is much more useful to use the words "I desire, intend, deserve and now gratefully accept."

If you have a "job," do not look to your job as your Source. If you do, the Universe can only give you what will fit through your paycheck. If you see your "job" as your mission, your calling and see God as the Source of your supply, you are then open to receive your abundance from billions of different directions, rather than just your paycheck.

We have within us everything we need to make our earthly incarnation a paradise if we choose to accept that which is our divine birthright. We live on a planet of abundance, although the majority of people focus on lack, scarcity and competition as if there does not exist enough for everyone.

LAW OF ACTION:

Action is imperative. Words are cheap; concepts and philosophies may be elegant, ideas may abound and good intentions sound impressive. Turning words, concepts and ideas into action requires energy; it requires sacrifice. It is better to do what we need to do than not do it and have good reasons or excuses. Most of us take action only when we feel motivated or the emotional, mental, or physical pain gets so bad we must act. Don't wait to feel motivated. Don't wait to get permission. Choose the way of courage and integrity, and act. The only time Humans have the ability to show courage is when they are afraid. If our heart confirms it, we should act, despite the feelings of fear, self-doubt, or insecurity; we should just do it. Action is stronger than subjectivity. No matter what we think or feel, we can still act.

The Universal Force has two fields of action – attraction and repulsion

– which transform into energy. In mechanical fields, force is recognized as energy; in psychological fields, as thought. Thought is a chemical action.

Action is the only thing that will accomplish anything. Without action, we have static or abortive ideas. Nothing is accomplished without action.

LAW OF AFFINITY OR LAW OF SOUL CONTRACT:

Before each incarnation we make decisions and a contract about what we and our soul wish to accomplish in each lifetime. We choose parents, race, sex and nationality. We choose time and place of birth in relationship to the astrological influences we wish to have. These influences can affect our character, personality, abilities, restrictions and timing for strengths or weaknesses. We choose certain individuals with whom we will feel an affinity when we meet them. We choose talents and occupations for which we will feel an affinity.

LAW OF AFFIRMATION:

Whatever we affirm for ourselves is the law of our being, our truth, whether we do this consciously or unconsciously. The subconscious mind takes what we affirm and acts on it without censorship, opinion or humor. The Subconscious and Super Conscious minds take our thoughts and emotions literally. If we use the term "I AM" before what we affirm, it is even stronger. Our conscious and subconscious both seek to align with and fulfill what we affirm.

LAW OF ALLOWANCE:

What we see as negative in another is also within our own being. We are called to allow each person the experience of his or her own choices without our judgment or condemnation. Judge not, lest you be judged, or condemn not, lest you be condemned. There is a difference between judgment and discernment. To discern a thing as not appropriate for us is correct. To say for example, "He is weak," could be discernment. To say, "He is weak and will always be weak," is a judgment. You have added your opinion of possible future behavior to your discernment of the situation you observed.

By the LAW OF FREEWILL we are required to allow everyone to make their own mistakes.

LAW OF APPROBATION:

Approbation means: the act of approving; approval, sanction. As we receive, we are to first approbate and then give out. We are to apply to our own lives that which we receive from our higher consciousness, and to prove it out, before we pass it on to others. No one learns by what we tell them. They learn only from observing what we are and what we demonstrate.

LAW OF ASCENSION:

To ascend is to rise up. We are in a constant state of raising our energy, or lowering it, by our thoughts and actions. It is possible for a person to ascend out of this dimension into another dimension at the time of their death. It is also possible to constantly raise our vibrations to be in a constant state of ascending into higher levels of consciousness through intention and meditation.

LAW OF ASPIRATION:

Desire and aspiration are not synonymous. To desire is to wish to obtain; to aspire is to achieve. Aspiration is the guiding power that directs the individual to strive for loftier goals. Aspiration elevates the individual beyond the plane of selfishness, and desire into the development of a pleasing personality and noble character. What we aspire to achieve, so far as our soul is concerned, we are capable of achieving. To wish and to aspire are not the same.

When we realize God rules the Universe under exact Law, we do well to aspire to a full understanding of these Laws and obedience to them. To aspire is similar to inspire. To be inspired is to be filled with spirit. Enthusiasm is to be filled with spirit.

En-theo-ism = filled with God.

LAW OF ASSOCIATION:

When two or more things have something in common, the commonality can be used to influence or control the other things. The amount of control depends on the degree of commonality. The more in common they are, the greater the influence. In a group of people who have a common goal or belief, the energy is exponentialized by the number in the group. The power of their energetic influence is much greater and the result of any action affects them all.

LAW OF ASSUMPTION:

Whatever we assume (take on) is ours. Our assumptions will make of us that which we assume. Do not assume the assumption of another. No person is required to take upon themselves the burden of another. We are all responsible for our own assumptions (our life experience). Each person is responsible for his/her life experience. To assume another's responsibilities does not help them to learn to carry their own load. It is always important to ask your own soul "Is this mine to do?" before we offer to assist others; it is important not to assume we know what is best for them.

LAW OF ATTITUDE:

Our own attitudes are the only things that can harm us. Our attitudes move us toward certain events and experiences, and it is our attitudes toward these experiences that will worsen or lighten any event, catastrophe or tragedy. We are always in control of our own attitude and how we will react or respond to any event.

LAW OF ATTRACTION:

What we focus on expands or appears. Where your attention goes, our energy flows. We attract what we are. We attract what matches our energy frequency, our thoughts and feelings. To achieve any given desire, idea, or goal, the consciousness *for it must first be established within us*. We attract what we concentrate upon. If we have negative thoughts, we will attract negative experiences. If we are loving and kind, we will experience loving kindness from others. We can attract to ourselves only those qualities we possess. To have peace and harmony in our life and in the World, we must have peace and harmony within ourselves. We attract things that match the frequency of our vibration. To have more and to be more, it is most important to focus on raising our own vibration.

LAW OF BALANCE:

All things in this dimension exist in a state of duality, which some see as balance: high and low, in and out, hot and cold, fast and slow, loud and soft; the interplay of opposites. Between the polarities rests a balance point, a center. The Earth exists in a state of balance. We are all energetically both male and female. We must pay equal attention to both sides to keep in balance the receptive nature and the projective nature. We have two hemispheres to our brains: a right brain and a left brain. Our left brain is logical and linear and thought of as masculine. Our right brain is abstract, non-linear and thought of as feminine or controlling our feeling nature. It is through the right brain that we can communicate with our souls. When we are truly balanced, it does not look like the yin/yang symbol of old, but looks energetically like three parts within the circle and represents our male/female/spiritual natures, the trinity. As long as we participate in duality, we are not balanced. True balance only comes from including spirit in our natures.

To balance and overcome duality, we must balance between:
Superiority and insecurity (knowing ourselves as divine beings)
Over-helping and resentful resistance or withdrawal (is this mine to do?)
Over-confidence and self-doubt (become soul-infused personalities)
Mind and emotions and spiritual energy
Analysis and disorientation (logic and intuition)
Extreme dependence and extreme independence (interdependence)
Idealism and disappointment
Naïve over-trusting and fear of betrayal
Passiveness and aggressiveness
Feast and famine
Puritanical and hedonistic tendencies
Work and rest and family

Taking care of ourselves and taking care of others
Our masculine and feminine natures
Giving and receiving

What we feel we need to receive is what we also need to give out.

LAW OF BEING:

We are spiritual beings and, as such, are governed by Spiritual Laws:
Our word is Law.
Our word creates.
Our word molds the physical body into either health or dis-ease.
As we think in our hearts, we are.
We live in our consciousness; there is nowhere else to live.
We make our own heaven or hell; our thinking makes it so.
Our thinking creates the vehicle for our soul.

LAW OF BELIEVING or KNOWING:

We must believe in ourselves as spiritual beings, having a Human experience, before we can understand the Laws that govern the Universe. We must know ourselves before we can transcend ourselves. All things are possible if we believe-know and nothing positive is possible unless we believe, know.

Until we remember the true definition of ourselves, we are operating from a place of not knowing. Our true definition is: "I AM God operating through the personality of (your name) for the benefit of Earth, all species of life on the Earth and beyond. This is the truth of who I AM." You can have anything you desire as long as you believe you can and as long as you believe you deserve it, and your having it will not harm another being.

To see is a third and fourth dimensional spiritual experience; to hear is a Third, Fourth and the lowest vibration of the Fifth dimension. Knowingness is a Fifth dimensional and higher dimensional experience.

LAW OF BODHISATTVA:

Bodhisattva is a Sanskrit term that means one who has transcended the need of Earthly incarnations but who has chosen to return to the Earth to support others in achieving enlightenment.

LAW OF CHARITY:

We are to be ever ready to help others to the fullest extent of our abilities, but ought not to interfere. Before even offering assistance, it is important to always ask our souls, "Is this mine to do?" We should help when we are asked, if our soul indicates it as ours to do, and we should always ask the person for their permission before assisting them. Charity in its right conception is not synonymous with mere giving, but is distinguished by discerning service, true helpfulness, kindness and love. Each person is a channel for the outflow of God's abundance to bless all Humankind. Again, it is important to ask our souls when it is correct for us to give or assist.

LAW OF CHOICE:

No matter what our circumstances, we have the power to choose what we think and feel. The most basic choice we have in life is whether to expand ourselves or to contract. We can choose whether to bring our creative, expressive energies into the World in positive or negative ways. Every choice we make takes us closer or further away from God. Every choice we make takes us closer to or further away from our heart's desires. The *LAW OF CHOICE* gives us the power to choose and the responsibility to choose how we will respond to our circumstances. Every choice has consequences; the fewer distorted or limiting beliefs we hold, the greater our power of choice. The more we honor the *LAW OF CHOICE*, the more clearly we can live our life on purpose and by choice, taking responsibility for our directions rather than viewing life as something that just happens to us. We have chosen the people and circumstances that are currently in our lives. We are free to make other choices. Everything that exists is made of energy. Energy can manifest itself as either positive or negative in relationship to our thoughts and choices.

Expressive energy, creative energy, demands release. We can release this energy through creative or destructive channels. We have the power of choice to use our expressive energy to lift up or tear down. We can learn to use our expressive energy in responsible and constructive ways. Once we agree to be a soul-infused personality, meaning to allow the soul to consciously use the body and to be involved in choice making, our lives are less stressful; choices become easier.

LAW OF COLOR OR THE RAYS:

The energies of The Rays express themselves on Earth as color. These Rays are Aspects of God - energy transmitted to Earth for use by Humans. Each Ray is sponsored and coordinated by a Master. The rainbow evidences these Rays. Now that there are 49 Rays of energy available to the Earth, it is not uncommon to see double rainbows. Any Human who is conscious of them may call upon them or call them forth. Colors can be used to increase or decrease the flow of certain streams of consciousness and energy. (For more information on the individual Rays, their meanings and uses, see *The 49 Rays: Their Meanings and Uses* **book channeled from the masters to bj King**, available from Namaste, Inc., P. O. Box 22174, Oklahoma City, OK 73123 (405)773-5210. The book with beautiful photographs is available from Amazon in digital format for $9.99 and from the website.

THE LAW OF COMMITMENT:

When we become clear in our commitment to our spiritual path and our desires, the Universe and our souls begin to work with us. To have multi-dimensional assistance requires commitment on our part.

LAW OF COMMUNION:

Our silver cord is our communication link with our Oversouls, our God-selves. The more in communion we are with our soul, the stronger our faith will become and the less alone we will feel. The more communions we have with our soul, the surer we feel about our direction and actions.

LAW OF COMPENSATION:

Any expenditure of energy produces a reaction; it is impossible for any action to take place without result. The reaction may not always be visible, or may not be measured by any of Earth's standards, but the reaction exists. Science says: "For every action there is a reaction, equal in force but opposite in nature." Every good has its compensation as well as every evil. Each Human is a law unto themselves, being both the giver and the receiver. We are always compensated in relationship to our thoughts, actions and beliefs. Because of the *LAW OF COMPENSATION*, we would do well to do unto others as we would have them do unto us. Since it may not always come from the direction we expect, we sometimes misperceive the compensation.

LAW OF CONFIRMATION:

How do we know a truth is a truth when we decide it is a truth? Law runs the Universe and it is constantly proving itself to us. This does not mean theory is not truth, but until we prove it to ourselves, it is still a theory. *THE LAW OF CONFIRMATION* is proof to us, not to someone else. When we open up spiritually, our bodies will give us confirmation when we've heard or read the truth, often by giving us chill bumps.

LAW OF CONSCIOUS DETACHMENT:

The Buddha taught, "It is your resistance to what is, that causes your suffering." By suffering, he meant everything that doesn't seem to be working in your life; relationship problems, loss of loved ones, loneliness, sickness, accidents, guilt, and monetary hardship, unfulfilled desires, etc. When you accept what is, you accept the unalterable realities in your life without resisting them. Some things are facts. They exist, and no matter how much you resist them, there is nothing you can do to be able to do anything about them. Change what you can change, but have the wisdom to accept what cannot be changed without wasting mental or physical energy attempting to change what you cannot change. Out of acceptance comes involved detachment. Develop the ability to enjoy all the positive aspects of life but allow the negative to flow through you without resistance and without letting it affect you.

LAW OF CONSCIOUSNESS:

Life is consciousness. Consciousness is the sum total of all our thoughts and feelings. We are in charge and we can, at any moment, change the outer picture we see. The World is not what it appears to be; it is what we believe it to be. We perceive the World according to our consciousness. It is what it appears to be to each of us. That does not mean that is the way it is. It only means that it is the way it appears to each of us through our individual filters of thought and belief. To achieve any given desire, ideal or goal, the consciousness for it must first be established within us. The building of consciousness is a divine activity. We rise to join God as co-creators, specifically the co-creator of our lives and desired good; only when our inner world changes will our outer World change.

When we live with the understanding life is consciousness, we can deal with cause, and we can change, adjust and transform. When we are ignorant of this Law, we deal with outer effects only. The development of physical awareness is needed to integrate the body, emotions and intellect into a harmonious conscious being, into a soul-infused personality.

Consciousness is not set in stone or predetermined; it is malleable. It can grow, expand and change. It can be transformed. As our inner awareness changes so will it affect our outer life. Getting in touch with and understanding our own thoughts and emotions leads to conscious awareness. To be fully conscious, we are required to activate and balance our right brain feeling nature with our left brain rational, objective nature. This allows attainment of Cosmic Consciousness. Consciousness is the cause of all effect.

**A conscious Human individual has the POTENTIAL
to be the highest, noblest cause for good in the Universe.**

LAW OF COURAGE:

Every Human being is endowed, according to their stage of evolution, with attributes of the soul such as love, faith, devotion, loyalty and unselfishness that stimulate the noblest form of courage. We are told by religion that spiritual courage is founded upon faith and unselfishness. Often it takes courage to be rationally selfish, to take care of our own welfare, our own time and energy, in order to have energy and time left to assist others.

It takes courage to say "no" when it is appropriate.

Courage is a vibratory emotion of a positive nature, and all souls within its sphere of radiation are attracted by it. When we face a dangerous or difficult situation courageously, we transmit the same feeling to others. By constant exercise of this positive attribute in meeting life's problems and adversities, we benefit not only ourselves, but all those whom we contact. We instill a matrix of courage into mass consciousness. When one person accomplishes an act of courage, whether it is facing danger or disease without fear, it adds that matrix to Human consciousness and makes it possible for others to accomplish acts of courage.

Courage is a great constructive power in overcoming the negative and destructive self-sabotaging forces within the self. It is an essential factor in self-control and self-discipline. Self-control and self-discipline do not mean self-repression; on the contrary, they spell power for self-expression gained through the exercise of courage in overcoming the self-sabotaging, self-destructive forces within and around us. Having the courage to examine our thoughts, beliefs and actions, and choosing to control them, is the highest Human calling. Controlling our thoughts and actions takes courage.

To love takes courage. To be a Human takes courage.

LAW OF CREATION:

Creation is energy, mind and essence. Our most powerful creative tools are thought and imagination. We are all creators in Human form. Our every word creates positively or negatively according to our thought patterns. Where our thoughts and attention go, the energy flows. We have the power to change anything we don't desire, but only by focusing on what we do desire.

Humans can create consciously and successfully only when our brains are connected to the Cosmic Mind – and the brain is not the Mind. The brain is merely the seat of sensation and the electric recorder of sensation. The brain is the receptor through which the Mind works. The person, who thinks inwardly to the Mind, can visualize or imagine that which spiritually exists, and then think outwardly through the senses and cause the mentally envisioned image to exist physically. Every genius thinks first inwardly toward their Mind.

LAW OF CYCLES:

Everything in the Universe is a form of energy and, therefore, everything falls within the *LAW OF CYCLES*. Sunrise and sunset, the waxing and waning of the moon, the ebb and flow of the tides and the seasons of the year all reflect this Law. All things have a most favorable and a least favorable time; all things rise and fall. Each of us has our own rhythms. As we find our own rhythm, we take advantage of whatever point of the cycle we find ourselves; we learn to flow in harmony and rhythm with the *LAW OF CYCLES*.

The World of nature exists within a larger pattern of cycles, such as day and night and passing of the seasons. The planets rotate in orbits or cycles and present new energies to the Earth. The Universe and the Galaxy operate in cycles, one planet depending on the others to stay in its cycle. The seasons do not push one another; neither do clouds race the wind across the sky; everything has a time to rise, and a time to fall. Whatever rises, falls, and whatever falls shall rise again; that is the principle of cycles. For more information, see Alan Cohn's *The Life you Were Born to Live* from New World Library.

LAW OF DHARMIC DIRECTION:

You have within you a guiding principle which is your duty to accomplish for yourself and society. Your Dharma is your work. You always have the free will not to fulfill your dharma, your contract. If you listen to your inner direction, it will direct you to fulfill your dharma and resolve your karma.

LAW OF DENIAL:

When you refuse to deal with highly emotional issues or refuse to take responsibility for your unpleasant situation, you avoid living up to your potential. Such things can be put off for lifetimes. But the effect will be experienced mentally, physically or as a lifestyle manifestation until you correctly balance the situation.

LAW OF DISCIPLINE:

The *LAW OF DISCIPLINE* points to a paradox. While freedom is our birth-right, it must be earned in this World; self-discipline remains the key to freedom and independence. This principle applies to both inner freedom and outer freedom. The focusing and discipline of inner practices, such as meditation, exploring our beliefs, and other insight work, can generate a sense of inner freedom and inner peace – breaking the chains of the brain/mind, the monkey mind that chatters uncontrolled.

Outer freedom expands as a result of our disciplined effort over time; such freedoms may include financial freedom associated with excellence in any field, greater mobility, the ability to travel, the freedom that comes with a strong healthy body; the social freedom, self-respect and satisfaction that come from disciplined labor; and in general, having more options in life. Discipline is a habit of doing just a little more, going just a little deeper, staying with something until we master it, pushing through it when it starts to be difficult; not giving up.

The *LAW OF DISCIPLINE* teaches us to set priorities and focus on one thing at a time until we get it right – focusing on the activities we need to do now and setting aside what we can do later. This question helps us to stay focused: What is the next single thing for me to do or know for me to be in a state of Divine Grace?

LAW OF DISCRIMINATION:

Being discriminating in thought and action brings about faith in self and faith in the Universe. The practice of discernment and discrimination are both paramount in developing spiritual mastery. Discernment is a spiritual gift and one can pray to their soul to receive discernment. I feel it is our most valuable spiritual gift. We are expected by our souls to discriminate between which of our thoughts should be acted upon and which are in need of correction.

LAW OF DISSIDENCE OR SELF-DELUSION:

We are going to experience mental discomfort when we hold two conflicting beliefs or when our actions do not agree with our beliefs. Examples would be: If a person believed smoking is bad for one's health and yet continued to smoke. To believe extramarital affairs are morally wrong and yet continue to be involved with someone other than one's spouse. When our beliefs and actions are incompatible, we will attempt to reduce the resulting discomfort by changing either our actions or our beliefs or by rationalizing our actions. The *LAW OF DISSIDENCE* is sometimes called the *LAW OF SELF-DELUSION* because the mind must either balance or rationalize actions.

LAW OF DIVINE LIFE AND PURPOSE:

We all come into this World beautiful, innocent, blessed, fully alive and encoded with spirituality. The journey of the soul is not linear. Life is a constant spiral of growth. Are we going in circles and spiraling downward through fear and belief in the illusion of mass consciousness and becoming pessimistic? Or are we choosing to spiral upward toward the soul and being optimistic? Our awe, wonder and wholeness must be nourished or it goes into hiding.

The purpose of each individual Human life is to recognize, use and to share our gifts, to prosper and to live happily. As with happiness, self-awareness cannot be given from one person to another. But by reflecting personal values, one can enhance another person's self-awareness in a similar way that one can enhance another person's happiness by example.

Having an illness can be judged as failure to demonstrate spiritual principles. We may feel guilty for having the disease. We would do well to ask ourselves, is this idea helpful? The process of looking for a corresponding state of mind to connect with various illnesses can give some insight, but, obviously, that insight is limited. We can have a genetic predisposition for a particular disorder. When the life force is diminished in us, or out of balance, we tend to be controlled by our worldly appetites, always desiring more, more, and more, whether it is food, sex, material goods, approval, love, acknowledgement or power. We must control our appetites rather than allowing them to control us.

Rid the mind of thoughts of disease. But, if a disease occurs, question its purpose in your life. What can I learn from this? Who can I meet, who can help me with this? Often the purpose of a physical problem is the soul's giving us an opportunity to take the body in front of healers, doctors, practitioners, who we need to meet or who need to meet us for some reason.

Guilting ourselves for developing a disease is not useful. Question what does it mean? What am I to learn from this? Where does the body desire to go for help? These are all useful questions when a disease appears in our bodies. We do well to affirm: I have a healthy life or I AM healthy, My life and body are healthy.

The Kundalini life force within us will awaken at the appropriate time; it should not be coerced. Forcing the Kundalini energy to rise can cause severe mental and emotional problems.

"I commit to awaken and to live life as a higher-order being."

LAW OF DIVINE ORDER:

If you seek to understand the *LAW OF DIVINE ORDER*, study the natural balance of nature, for it works very much the same way. Everything is as it should be, although Humankind is far from experiencing its potential of total harmony. There are no accidents. Your energy, translated into thoughts, words, motions and deeds, causes all your experiences. This assures you always have the learning opportunities you require to resolve your karma; and, as with you, the collective thoughts, words, motions and deeds of Humankind create the environment for us all.

If enough souls focus their energy upon peace, we will have peace. If the majority of souls are filled with anger, we may all have to experience war. We are all one, and like the many sub-personalities within you, the dominant traits of Humankind will emerge to resolve our group karma. At this moment, a born-again Christian Evangelist preaches fear from a pulpit in West Virginia, while a Yoga instructor directs a loving group meditation in Oregon. One is directing the energy of the gestalt into disharmony, the other into harmony. Hopefully, at least one can cancel out the other. If we can't obtain harmony, maybe we can balance the disharmony. Fear is the problem. Love is the answer.

LAW OF DOMINANT DESIRE:

A strong emotion will always dominate a weaker one. Every idea you perceive is the beginning of a manifestation, although all ideas are not expressed in reality. It doesn't matter which idea you consciously favor or even know to be desirable – the stronger emotion will nullify the weaker ones and the strongest emotion will begin to permeate all aspects of your activities.

LAW OF DUALITY:

The Universe and all energy functions as a Yin/Yang balance, resulting in a tension between opposites. Yin is negative, Yang is positive. We all contain these dual aspects expressed as love and hate, harmony and chaos, good and evil. This tension is necessary for structure to exist. Humans are energy structures. Don't be mistaken and think in terms of negative being bad. An automobile battery is a good analogy. One plate is charged positively and the next negative, the next positive and so on. It is the interaction between the plates that generate the energy, but the negative plate is not better than the positive plate. In relating this to your life, you must realize without tension you don't exist; thus, there is a need for Yin balance in your life. Most people express their Yin energy in undesirable ways such as self-denial, excessive hard work, gambling, dangerous activities such as driving too fast or in arguing or fighting. Illness is an expression of Yin energy and war is the ultimate expression of mass Yin energy. But your Yin energy can be expressed in a different way, as a positive challenge.

LAW OF DUTY:

Duty gets its moral quality in relation to the individual will and impulse. Duty is largely an individual matter, for what is regarded as a moral obligation for one person may not be so regarded by another. We have a spiritual duty to cease all mental and spiritual action that interferes with growth of positive character and, as far as possible, to make our physical conditions or surroundings conform to the best interest of progression. It is our duty to utilize our powers to assist others and ourselves to develop our own higher self to meet the challenges of life. We are to seek knowledge and understanding of the Laws governing our own being – body, mind and soul – and to obey them, thus becoming an outlet or channel for Divine expression.

Each one of us is equipped and spiritually assigned a job to be done in this World; a mission in life, a duty to be performed to the best of our ability. We chose these assignments before we entered this incarnation. It matters not to God or the World whether we are a butcher or a bishop, but it matters whether we are the best butcher or the best bishop we are capable of being.

LAW OF ENVIRONMENTAL MANIFESTATION:

Everything that surrounds you is an extension of you. Your mate, your home, your furnishings, your car, your pets, your yard, your office and your career are a physical expression of your attitudes and belief systems. Your environment is a reality picture of your core belief and expresses your self-image and cultural overview.

LAW OF EXCHANGE:

The Law states: "If an individual utilizes and exercises the energies of sharing with another Human being, then they must make themselves available and open to receive like energies in return."

This is one of the most difficult Laws for Humankind to observe properly. We are brought up from childhood to learn to "give and take." There should only be sharing. The word "give" involves a form of sacrifice. The word "take" implies drawing to one's self without permission. If one wishes to return energies to you, to share with you, you are not taking, you are receiving. You are allowing others to exercise the same vibrat ions you yourself have exercised, and you have no right to deny them this. The Law encourages us to share. In this manner, the recipient is able to receive a greater portion of energies without any loss of strength, stability or self-ownership.

"It is every individual's responsibility to own him or herself totally. When one attempts to 'give of himself' to another, he opens himself to vulnerability and may create karma."

LAW OF EXPECTATION:

What we expect is what we get. What we truly believe will happen, will happen. This is not about what we think, but about what we truly believe. If we believe we are victims of fate, we believe in something outside ourselves creating our reality. We always create events based on our expectations and beliefs. Worry places energy into the creation of what we do not desire; when we worry, we are giving all our power for what we don't desire to happen.

LAW OF EXPERIENCE:

New information entering your mind destroys previous information of a similar nature. Once the pathway of information has been established in your brain, that viewpoint will prevail unless new information comes in to destroy and replace it. As an example: While horseback riding, you fall off and hurt yourself. Now, if that is the end of your experience with horses, your experience has been programmed negatively. That is why instructors always encourage new riders to climb back aboard immediately after falling off. You need fresh, new input to erase the trauma of the fall. The Law is an innate, organic process and does not require your conscious attention or active participation. It suggests the basic processes of the brain are in an endless state of growth and reorganization. Now, the *LAW OF EXPERIENCE* can be used effectively in an altered state of consciousness programming because your subconscious cannot tell the difference between fantasized experience and a real experience. As an example: If you always feel extreme anxiety in crowds – in an altered state you could vividly imagine yourself perfectly relaxed in a crowd of people and the mind will accept this as a reality and invoke the *LAW OF EXPERIENCE*. After a few days, weeks or months of this programming, your mind will have totally experienced being calm in crowds and it will carry over into your personality.

LAW OF FAITH:

If we believe in a benevolent Universe, the Universe supports us in a positive way. If we align our energy and intention and allow Spirit to join us through faith that Spirit exists and can work through us instead of relying only on our own will power and stamina, we are practicing faith. The Universal energy flowing through us is the Source of our life and breath and heartbeat. The Universal energy is infinitely at our disposal through simply plugging in to faith, with our heart's desire defined. Until we create the perfect conditions for a miracle, through our faith, there won't be a miracle. The power of the Universe is at our disposal but we must believe it and plug in; just like to have light, we must believe in electricity. The energy of the Universe is like electricity; if we have a lamp and do not plug it into an electrical outlet and turn it on, it will not light up and become functional.

The struggle with faith is that we have forgotten we are souls. We are disconnected from the truth of our existence. In truth, we are God operating through these bodies and personalities. We often grow to believe we are our bodies or the roles we play; we forget our Divine origins.

LAW OF FEARFUL CONFRONTATION:

This Law says if you fear doing something, and yet have the courage to do it anyway, you will soon do a mental flip-flop and may even become addicted to doing it. As an example: If you fear skydiving, but force yourself to do it, the experience generates the internal release of beta endorphins. These internally manufactured opiates chemically resemble Opium, and are quite addicting. The more you skydive, the more you will desire to skydive or ski straight down mountains or gamble or whatever it was that you originally feared and it still causes you an internal rush.

LAW OF FELLOWSHIP:

When two or more people of similar vibration are gathered for a shared purpose, their combined energy directed to the attainment of that purpose is raised exponentially in relationship to the number of people. This acroamatic awareness has been used by covens, esoteric religions, healing groups and, recently, Worldwide meditations for World peace.

LAW OF FLEXIBILITY:

Flexibility involves a pragmatic acceptance of, rather than rigid resistance toward, the present moment – acceptance of ourselves, others, and current circumstances. This does not in any way imply passive toleration for what we don't like, nor does it mean ignoring injustice or allowing ourselves to be victimized. Flexibility requires an alert and expansive state of awareness; it entails not just "going with the flow", but embracing and making constructive use of it. Mastering the *LAW OF FLEXIBILITY*, we can turn stumbling blocks into stepping-stones and problems into opportunities. Flexibility avails us far more than either passivity or resistance; by actively using whatever arises, embracing even the most painful circumstances, we deal with our difficulties more effectively as we begin to see them as a form of spiritual training. To live in a constant state of resistance invariably causes us to suffer.

No one can be forgiven unless they are willing to first forgive themselves. There can be no healing without forgiveness.

LAW OF FORGIVENESS:

It has become popular these days to blame almost everything on our childhoods, our parents, how we were raised, our abusers and our supposed role models. It has become popular to go to encounter groups, self-help groups and anonymous groups of all sorts. We do this in order to look at our "stuff", what we are still carrying with us, that which holds us back, that which makes us fearful. We have decided that if our childhoods had been different we would be full of self-love and self-confidence. We seem to be seeking a reason that our self-esteems are so low. We seem to be a civilization specializing is self-loathing. The abuse we suffered in the past is nothing compared to what we are heaping on ourselves now. We are desperately seeking a "method", a group, a philosophy, a diet, a drug, a relationship, which will either make us forget or make it possible for us to at least "cope" with the state of our own psyches. We attend seminars, we relate, we emote, we rebirth, we allow ourselves to be Rolfed, massaged and encountered to try to get to the bottom of our "issues".

We seem to be trying to find a reason outside ourselves to blame for the state of our insides. What most of us experience inside is fear and anxiety; fear of failure and fear of success; fear of being known and fear of being unknown; fear of intimacy and fear of never finding someone with whom we can be intimate. We go through relationships and sometimes marriages repeatedly. We play the same roles over and over with different people, with different costumes and different scripts in different settings with the same outcomes. Until one day it dawns on us, somehow, no matter where we go and whom we encounter, we are there and there is still the problem; i.e., "we" must be the problem. We then have reason to hate ourselves even more. Jesus said, "Love your neighbor as yourself." Often, we find it easier to love our neighbor than to love ourselves.

The truth is the past is over. It doesn't matter who we think we are, who we were, what anyone did to us, how our parents treated us or didn't treat us, or how much we have been ignored. If we are ready to change, help is available in an instant. We can continue to look at what happened and try to mentally and emotionally figure out why it happened and how we feel about it, or we can decide to get on with our lives. We can stay stuck in processing blame, guilt and fear or we can ask for help from our Source, which has the power to help us. First, we have to be ready and willing to be different. We have to be willing to change. We can look at our "stuff" forever; we can blame forever; we can feel shame forever; we can stay guilty; or we can ask for, receive and accept forgiveness and get on with our lives.

We are spiritual beings who came to Earth to live within Human bodies to co-create with God by extending love. We were born innocent; we were born with love to offer. We were dipped in a bath of forgetfulness as we left the spiritual dimension in order to be able to tolerate the shock of coming into a body. The memory of where we are from is still with us when we arrive; vague, but present. We love everyone. When we entered a body, that body was immersed in the mass consciousness. The mass consciousness contains fear. We learned fear after we arrived here. We came into this World where fear is being practiced as the norm and, therefore, we accepted it as normal and began to practice it with everyone else. We forgot where we came from and why we came. We accepted a role in the Human drama or soap opera of Earth. The script we were handed read, "act guilty, be competitive, struggle, get sick, there's not enough of everything for everybody, you are bad because you were conceived in sin, you will die, don't get attached to anything because you will lose it or it will die, above all else protect yourself at all times, because people want to harm you." We become a part of a cast playing out roles in a sea of free-floating fear and, therefore, we suffer from non-specific anxiety.

I have yet to meet anyone who wasn't from a dysfunctional home of some kind. I have yet to meet anyone who isn't practicing some form of dysfunction, whether it is self-loathing, self-sabotage, co-dependency, drinking, doing drugs, eating disorders, gambling, obsessive/compulsive disorder, control, sex, violence or illness. Emotional energy has to go somewhere. Self-hatred and fear are powerful emotions; so are love, hope and joy.

Our Spirit and Love are still within us. They may be buried from our conscious minds by guilt, anger, fear and self-hatred. Love is energy. Joy is energy. They cannot be seen or bought. The "feelings" of love and joy are responses to these energies. If we choose to accept this as a truth, we can go directly to God, Jesus, or the Holy Spirit and ask to be healed of our fears and self-loathing. We can decide to forgive others and ourselves. We can ask for a miracle or we can continue to suffer and pretend we don't know what causes us to feel fear. We can continue to blame our parents for our lack of love, our feelings of shame and continue to believe we were "victims" of abuse.

I do not believe there are any victims. I believe in the Universal Law of Karma, the Law of Cause and Effect. Something might appear or feel like victimization to us, but my experience is when we look at it from a universal viewpoint, from the point of the soul, it can be explained. The <u>Universal Laws are impersonal</u>. I do not believe in a vengeful or judgmental God who lets people suffer, starve or be homeless. I believe there is enough of everything for everyone on the planet. God does not let people starve; people let people starve. People control the supply. Economically, it is not feasible to give food away to people who are not paying for it. Economically, it is not feasible to give housing to people who are homeless, even though there are thousands of empty houses all over the World and warehouses full of food. Economics must be served or, according to the experts, we would have chaos. Left to itself, nature does not produce chaos. The Universal Laws do not produce chaos. People in control produce chaos.

I also believe we cannot solve a problem at the level or vibration at which it was created. It can only be transmuted by a higher vibrational solution or energy. We cannot solve a problem or condition by being at war with it or by getting into a state of opposition. This increases the energy of the problem or condition. We cannot make war on drugs or violence without increasing the resistance and, thereby, giving energy to it. We cannot fight for peace, change what is happening to dolphins or endangered species by opposing anyone or anything. We can only become a part of the solution by praying and by being conscious. By changing our own consciousness, we change the consciousness of the collective. When we oppose or fight against anything, we stay a part of the problem. We can claim our power and the Christ authority, the Dominion we were given by God. (Dominion refers to a level of the Angelic realm – caregivers, not to have dominion, as in control.) We were given free will and energetically we can change the vibrations of various situations through the use of our minds, our consciousness. As a species, we individually and collectively need miracles, and miracles do exist. Miracles are available if we ask and believe.

People stay in dysfunctional relationships because they fear not being O.K., being alone or not being able to support themselves. It allows them to be dependent and to avoid emotional responsibility for their lives. Forgiveness of self and others frees our mind and restores it to peace; it offers us miracles.

"I now forgive myself for all known and unknown limitations I have placed upon myself and others."

To NOT forgive another person is like taking poison and expecting the other person to die. Not forgiving the other person holds us in bondage to them and gives them power over us.

LAW OF FREE WILL:

Matthew: *"As we have stated, we, as Humans, were given 'free will' by our Creator. This experiment included the possibility Humans would not use this LAW to their own advantage, because they would not understand it. THE LAW OF FREE WILL includes the free will to 'think' anything we choose. The 'choice' is ours. We also have the ability to abdicate our 'free will' in favor of the 'will of the soul' or 'Divine Will' or 'God's Will,' but even if we turn our will over to the soul or to God, we still have free will. As Jesus did in his prayer, 'Thy kingdom come, Thy will be done, on Earth as it is in Heaven...' He abdicated His will to the Will of his Father, or the Divine Will. Some individuals today and in the past have more or less sold their free will to others in exchange for being cared for and some have been taken over as slaves, relinquishing their free will to an authority who threatened to take their physical life if they did not obey. The truth is even in these situations these individuals still had the free will choice of thought. If they had understood the Universal Law, thoughts are things; they could have overridden their seeming authorities' hold over them."*

Many people, as I was, have been afraid to turn their will over to God for fear they would be asked to do something they did not desire to do. God never takes our free will, even when we consciously turn our will over to Him. I turned my will over to God out of desperation, not realizing my vehicle had been created by God and had in all reality always been God's, except I had been given the free will choice of how to use it. Once I had turned my will over to God, God asked me, "What do you desire to do? Where do you desire to be?" I was shocked when He said, "You will find My Will for your life will very closely parallel your own heart's desires."

For years I followed the messages I received from my soul, thinking they were orders because I had said to God, "I will go anywhere, say anything, do anything you ask, if you will only talk to me." Finally, $26,000 in debt, most of which was at 21% interest, I threatened to quit following the instructions. The soul then said to me, "These were never orders, these were always suggestions. You always retain your free will. When you receive a suggestion from your soul it is always important to remember you can say, 'No' or you can write out 'conditions under which I can do that are:' and list your conditions. If it is important to the soul, the suggestion be accomplished through you, you will begin to see your conditions fulfilled and you can proceed." I was furious I had not been told sooner that these were suggestions and not orders. The soul then explained how to clear the debt and within a year, I was still homeless, but I was also debt-free.

We are not now, nor have we ever been, separated from our Source – God. Because of the *LAW OF FREEWILL*, we have the power to deny this truth as our personal reality. We can maintain our ignorance by denial. We are capable of uniting with THE God Mind, joining in consciousness to create the kind of lives of which we have only dreamed.

LAW OF GENEROSITY:

True generosity, like love, is a quality of the soul. Deeds of the Spirit are performed without any thought or hope of gain or reward and cannot be compensated for in terms of the material. If we give to the World the best we have, our best selves, the best will come back to us. It is important to never do for others what they are unwilling to do for themselves. It is a violation of this Law to be kind to one person at the expense of another. Generosity is a quality of love that gives of itself without any expectation of a material reward, the giving grants true freedom. Each time we give, we are actually proving to ourselves that we have.

LAW OF GRACE:

Karma can be experienced to the letter of the Law or in mercy and grace. In other words, if you give love, mercy and grace to others, you will receive the same in return. Example: You have destined a future event of which you will be the victim of slander and gossip which will ruin your career, but, in the years preceding this event, you have become so kind and loving to other Human beings it is obvious to your higher self you have learned your needed lesson, so the predestined event will be mitigated to the point of having little or no effect upon you. Example: In a previous lifetime, you were a person of great wealth which you used selfishly for your own and your family's indulgence. In this life you have destined yourself to experience monetary need, but you were so giving with the little you have, you have released yourself from this self-imposed bondage and once again will rise monetarily, always sharing what you have with those in need. It is a good idea to pray for grace from your soul daily.

LAW OF GRATITUDE:

To be grateful for what we already have blesses it and us. For every accomplishment and good that enters our lives we are to consciously give thanks. For every positive, progressive step we take in our lives, we are to give thanks. When we express gratitude for all that comes to us, more abundance of good comes to us. Even in being grateful for the lessons of life that come as struggle can we increase our consciousness. In addition to being grateful, it is useful to be appreciative. Appreciation and gratitude are similar, but to have appreciation involves our senses, where gratitude is a mental function. To be grateful for the rain is different than appreciating the feel and smell of the moisture when it is happening.

LAW OF GRAVITY:

Gravity is the magnetic force which causes objects to be drawn toward the center of the Earth and causes the planets, stars, our Sun and our Moon to remain in orbit.

LAW OF GROUP CONSCIOUSNESS:

Every one of us is a part of a great energy gestalt and connected on the level of the galactic unconscious. Each individual aspect of the gestalt has its own electrical system, its own vibrational frequency and interacts with all other aspects. Thus, we are all electrically connected to one another and to a central point. On a higher self or psychic level, it is possible for anyone to tune in to anyone else and to draw upon the awareness of the entire gestalt. Like the concept of the 100th monkey, Humankind takes advancing steps when group consciousness reaches a critical mass and new awareness is accepted by the whole.

LAW OF GROWTH:

Deep within our center, the level of higher self, we know what is best for us. It will always be to strive for more awareness. Never allow yourself to reach a level of self-satisfaction where there is no new challenge. For most of us, there will be no growth without agitation or discontent, so the idea is to carefully study your dissatisfactions for they will tell you what you are about to leave behind and possibly point to new future directions. Make sure the future is one of happiness and success.

LAW OF HARMONY:

When the physical, mental, emotional and spiritual are all balanced and operating in our lives, we will be in a state of harmony. THE *LAW OF HARMONY* will be in operation in our lives. Disharmony or dis-ease is a result of being out of balance in one area of our lives. When we come into closer harmony with our Soul, then the energy of Love and the expression of Love increase. Love creates harmony.

LAW OF HONESTY:

Honesty entails action in line with higher Laws despite negative impulses to the contrary. Recognizing, accepting, and expressing our authentic interior reality lies at the heart of honesty. Only when we are honest with ourselves can we speak or act honestly with anyone else. The *LAW OF HONESTY* points to higher Laws and inner consequences, which are instant, inevitable, and inescapable. We cannot truly deceive anyone but ourselves.

When we are dishonest in any way, with ourselves or with others, intentionally or not, our internal parts fight one another and our inner sense of spirit or inspiration fades; we feel cut off and alone and we attract whatever lessons we need to learn. Concepts of morality may change, but consequences are absolute.

LAW OF HOPE:

"Christ in you, the hope of glory." (Colossians 1:27) Glory can be defined as a state of richness, abundance and overflowing beauty. The hope of glory, esoterically thinking, is the reflection upon our mind of a reality which exists deep within our Inner Being. It is the possibility that will manifest or actualize when enough effort is put forth. Hope is the magnetic pull of that reality which is on the verge of manifestation. Hope mobilizes all our physical, emotional, mental and spiritual energies to make the reality (which is hoped for) actualize itself. Hope must be combined with THE *LAW OF ACTION* for results to materialize.

Each achievement of a person is a result of the attraction between hope and God. As a person gets closer to God, they manifest greater beauty, greater creativity and greater wealth of wisdom and power.

Hope is a spring through which the healing waters of God flow. That is why we say hope heals; hope gives light, strength, striving, persistence and patience. Hope is an inherent capacity of the Human soul, hope in the immortal evolution of life. The hope of Human immortality constitutes one of the greatest stabilizing forces for all Humankind.

Hoping for an outcome or wishing for an outcome does not replace asking for help from our soul and following the actions suggested by our souls.

LAW OF IMMACULATE CONCEPTION:

Each person is the immaculate concept of Infinite Intelligence. That spark of divinity within Humankind, the God within, is immaculate. Immaculate

Conception means those created through love. All are created through the love of The Creator.

LAW OF INCREASE:

All things increase with use. We can have nothing except what we hold in our consciousness. If we are rich in consciousness, it will express in our lives as abundance. If I say, "I desire wealth", but focus my thoughts on my debt or unpaid bills, rather than on "How can I increase my income today?" I am ignoring the *UNIVERSAL LAW OF INCREASE*, which is: What we focus our energy on increases.

Energy follows intention. Energy does not have a mind of its own; it follows our intention. It does not question, censor or decide for us, "Was that a conscious intention, a habitual thought, or a subconscious intention that Human just had?" It just automatically flows to fulfill or carry out the intention or thought. It flows with the speed and force of the emotion behind the Human thought.

LAW OF INCREASING ORDER:

When a point of limit is reached, some entities co-operate to transcend the limit. In so doing, they evolve into the next stage of life, which displays greater complexity, consciousness, freedom and order. In consonance with the *LAW OF INCREASING ORDER*, to keep reproducing ourselves, we must eventually transcend ourselves.

LAW OF INTUITION:

Intuition means "inner teacher". Intuition is not random nor is it a fluke. It is a true connection of one's Super Conscious Mind to their conscious mind. Divine consciousness is constantly seeing ways to express itself through us. It will respond to our desire and intention to be in commu-nication with our souls. Spiritual guidance, intuition, comes in the form of a sixth sense. Intuition, spiritual guidance, can be received at any time by anyone. We are required to expand our mental awareness in order to receive inner guidance. It requires an intention to quiet the mind's chatter and to turn our focus inward toward our heart, the seat of our soul. This can be done through meditation, movement exercise or any repetitive action, which frees the mind.

The *LAW OF INTUITION* can provide a needed leverage for those who come into this World without a strong sense of identity, center or inner direction. It also addresses the needs and issues of those who tend to feel very sensitive to criticism and who worry about whether they are doing the right thing, which often gets defined by someone else. What others think of us is really none of our business.

When we look outside ourselves for authority, we allow that authority to overshadow the wisdom of our own hearts. We can't get in touch with our heart while we're monitoring others' opinions. All outside opinions need to be checked out against our innermost feelings -- our own heart wisdom. Most people have inner guidance whether they call it a hunch, intuition, a feeling, the collective unconscious, archetypes, inner wisdom, spirit guides or God self.

Spirit has said intuition can come in visions, dreams, a voice or knowing. Visions and dreams are of the slowest vibration of Spirit. Auditory is the next higher level of Spirit communication. Knowingness is the higher form of Spiritual or soul communication. I recommend asking your soul for the gifts of discernment and knowing. Most of us came into this life from a high enough vibration that our souls would prefer that we not lower our vibrations to seeing and hearing. Once you ask for knowingness, the messages you receive can be much clearer. Your intuition can come as a full-bodied knowingness as if you saw it and heard it.

Allow yourself to feel in your heart, your sense of purpose and direction. Ask to know.

LAW OF JOY:

Joy is energy. Love is energy. Hope is energy. These are energies and qualities we can ask for from our soul. There is no courage without joy. Joy radiates from courage. Joy is a special wisdom. It keeps the vision of the achievement present in the eye of the person creating, providing steady inspiration for their efforts.

The Master El Morya says: "Joy heals the wounds received on the path of a courageous life. Joy disperses any negative accumulation in the aura of the courageous one. It builds a shield around the person through which all of the arrows of the adversary cannot penetrate. Joy changes bitterness into love; it nourishes the nerves and strengthens the heart. Joy gives the quality of positivity to all our actions on all personality levels. Never was a command rejected when it was given with joy. Joy carries the command to our Innermost Center. Joy is the manifestation of the Creator's Power, illuminating a World of darkness."

LAW OF JUSTICE:

The *LAW OF JUSTICE* deals justice to all alike. God does not punish us. We are punished or rewarded by the *LAW OF JUSTICE* for acts and thoughts of wrongdoing or acts of benevolence. It is equal to the *LAW OF KARMA*.

LAW OF KARMA – LAW OF CAUSE AND EFFECT:

Life begins within and then is projected outward into the picture (reality) of our lives, because Cause always precedes Effect. What we think is what we get.

Everything that goes around comes around. What we sow is what we reap. If we plant spinach, we will not get wheat. Nature is a manifestation of God. Nature gives of its all in every action and re-gives equally in every reaction. Nature always gives equally, for God always gives equally. Unless we first give, we will not be re-given.

If we speak into a tape recorder, what we hear will be exactly what we said. The results of the thoughts we send out come back to us magnified by our intent. The power of emotion causes the thought to be projected with force and, thereby, will exist in the ethers for an extended period of time.

Meditation is an expression of desire for knowledge of perfect Cause for the purpose of producing perfect Effect, to multiply God-awareness in our self. Meditation is for the purpose of remembering our immortality.

If we defy Universal Law to the slightest extent it will hurt us equally. If we work with Universal Law it will work with us to the fulfillment of our every desire.

LAW OF KARMIC EXCESS:

Karma incurred in one incarnation could be so overwhelmingly harmonious or disharmonious to have it all return in one lifetime would put you out of balance. Therefore, it is dispersed or worked out in more than one incarnation.

LAW OF KINDNESS:

Kindness is a quality of charity and an attribute of love. The person who has risen above such destructive traits as greed, selfishness, hatred, jealousy, envy, and has evolved to the plane where generosity, patience, tolerance, sympathy and love radiate from his every thought, word and deed – such an individual is obeying the laws of their soul and embodies in their character and personality the essence of kindness. The *LAW OF KINDNESS* extends, also, to the forms of life lower than the Human. In our relations with all forms of life, it is our duty to love and to help, to be kind and to co-operate in promoting the welfare of all of God's creation. All are part of One Life. We must work in harmony with, not against, the *LAW OF NATURE*.

LAW OF LIFE:

As we give to life, life gives back to us.

LAW OF LOVE:

God is Love. Love is the great cosmic adhesive, the greatest form of energy. Love is the basis of Spirit. The *LAW OF LOVE* is the basis of creation. Love is not a commodity or a feeling; it is our essence. Love and Light are synonymous. Light is pure, raw power awaiting our direction. When we claim the *LAW OF LOVE* for ourselves and take back our power, doors that have been closed, open; minds that have been closed, open. We have the freedom to experience limitless joy, kindness, passion, union, compassion, synergy, happiness, bliss, delight, peace and wonder. We can feel truly powerful.

If we send Love before us it will bring unity and harmony in all situations. Love will dissolve all that is not in harmony. God is Love and we are the instruments using love as a means of Self-expression and Self-actualization.

Love shows the way
Love always has an answer
Love always is the answer
Love has within it the seed of resolution
Give out love to inspire others to re-give love.

Mastering anything is the fruit of love. The Soul alone can give out love. The body can render a perfect technical reproduction, but if the love nature of God is not in us, it is not truly inspired art, for inspired art is the skill of rendering a visible or audible thing in the beauty and love that only the stillness of the Light of our soul can give it.

Love must be interwoven in every stitch of whatever pattern we are weaving, every word we are writing and every interchange between us and others. The quality of our material interpretation lies in our ability to translate imagined forms and rhythms of the Universal heartbeat into physical forms and rhythms that can re-inspire others with the ecstasy of our inspiration.

When we inspire others, we are manifesting the love nature of God and the fulfillment of the *LAW OF LOVE* by giving love. Love is the nature of God. Open your inner door and let your God Self in – before you begin your day – your creation.

Whatever good we behold in another person must also live in us as well. Those who appreciate art have a hidden artist within them. They may be afraid to express their own talent because they are comparing themselves and their vision to that of others. In every situation, we are either coming from love or we are coming from fear.

Some part of us remembers the energy of love. An ancient memory of this love haunts all of us all the time. We have a sense of desiring to "go home" to that memory. We seek to feel that feeling again by "falling in love" by becoming involved in relationships which never quite fulfill that yearning because they are a substitute for what we are really seeking. What I believe we are really seeking is to reestablish our communion with GOD. When we entered the Earth plane, we became a part of a mass consciousness which believes in separation, a consciousness in which the majority believe they are separate from God. There is no way to be separate from God. Our heartbeat is a direct impulse of God's love for us. ***I let Love flow*** *in and out of my life as my breath.*

We cannot fulfill our contracts, our soul's desires, without consciousness of our Source. God's creation is Nature, for God is Love and Love is what Nature is.

When the genius of your Soul sends out a visible or audible message, which awakens the genius in another Soul and re-inspires them with your inspiration, you have extended your immortality to another. By your inspiration, you awaken them to their genius, their immortality. You have uplifted their cultural standard and in so doing, have uplifted the cultural standard of all of Humankind. Your transcendent genius is the result of your communion with God. Align your heartbeat with the rhythm of the Universal heartbeat, become in tune with the Infinite.

Meditation is communion with God for the purpose of acquiring knowledge and power to manifest with God as Co-Creator of His Universe in order to enable the Mind to control matter.

LAW OF MAGNETISM:

Like attracts like. True magnetism is the ability to receive psychic energy throughout our auras, to receive impressions coming from higher sources, which enrich our lives and make us successful in all aspects of our lives. What we think about, we magnetize into our lives.

LAW OF MANIFESTATION:

Every manifestation begins as an idea. Our minds have unlimited creative power to manifest. After the "idea" must come dedication, awareness, training and following spiritual guidance to turn an idea into a physical reality. We were created to be creators and given free will to think as we will. What we think becomes our reality. What we give conscious thought and energy to becomes our fastest reality. Worry causes that which we worry about to happen. Positive thought and positive action create a positive, enjoyable life.

LAW OF MATERIALIZATION:

The *LAW OF MATERIALIZATION* is technically bringing Spirit into matter through intent and concentration. Materialization is the Law that says a thought held in mind strongly enough, with intention, will become material or physical. That which we imagine might materialize in the outer. First, there must be a perfect mental concept of the thing as a physical reality. Know that whatever we can conceive, we can achieve.

LAW OF MIND:

THOUGHTS ARE THINGS

**"Thoughts held in our mind become our reality.
Thoughts held in our mind produce after their kind."**

Matthew: "*Jesus concerned Himself with the teaching of general principles and these general principles always had to do with mental states, for He knew if one's mental state is right, everything else must be right, too; whereas, if it is wrong, nothing else can be right. There is a Cosmic Law that nothing can permanently deny its own nature. If a person does good deeds outwardly, but holds malice in their heart, that which returns to them will be an out-picturing of their thoughts and feelings. If gifts are given with the thought of return, desire for gratitude, or to cause the giver to appear generous, that which is returned to them again will be the out-picturing of their thoughts and not their actions. What goes on in the mind and the intention behind the thoughts is the cause of an individual's reality.*"

We can't plant tomato seeds and expect to grow asparagus. Our thoughts are seeds we are always planting. We are what we think about all day long. Our present life is being created moment by moment by our thoughts and feelings. We have a responsibility to think kind, loving, abundant thoughts. We have a responsibility to be happy, to create the good, the beautiful and the holy.

Life is a direct result of our consciousness. We are expected to embrace our divine potential in order to clear our consciousness and to elevate our sense of worthiness. We must first create a consciousness within for anything we wish to experience in our outer reality.

We can have anything we truly desire. We can attract anything we set our heart and mind upon. Past, painful experiences must cease to be the creative energy of our lives.

The kind of life we are living reflects our consciousness. Consciousness is the sum total of all our thoughts and feelings. The principle of consciousness teaches us that we are in charge of our destiny and that at any moment we can change our thoughts, our perceptions and, thereby, change our reality.

A peaceful perception of the World can arrive only from a peaceful mind. A peaceful mind can result only from the consistent planting of thoughts of peace; only when our inner World changes can our outer World change.

We must clear our consciousness and elevate our sense of worthiness. We can accomplish this by embracing our divine potential. When we understand life is consciousness, we can change, adjust and transform – by dealing with "cause", which is thought. When we are ignorant of the Law, thoughts are what create effects. We can continually manipulate effects and our situation is not going to change permanently, because consciousness is the cause of all effect. We must first observe our thoughts and ourselves in order to change our thoughts.

God has given us the power to create through thought. We always have choice. We have free will. We can decide whether to use our power constructively or destructively. We can choose to give it away or to empower ourselves. The power of the divine fills each of us, and all we need to do is claim it. Claiming it means no longer leading with our wounds. Only we can imprison ourselves; only we can set ourselves free.

When we create fear or drama, it gives us an adrenaline rush. We know we are alive. If we talk about how awful it is to everyone we encounter, or rehash it ourselves, it gives power to the negative. When a disturbing thought comes into our minds, we would do well to stop, replace it with a positive, true, life-affirming thought.

Until we open to this spiritual reality, we believe all we see with our physical eyes is the totality of possibility. What we see is our perception, which is based on some very limited information. Transformed perception leads to seeing into a higher reality. We must first observe ourselves, and our thoughts, in order to change them. What we focus on expands.

Affirm: I am willing to see myself, other people, things and situations differently.

The World doesn't just happen; it is a result of an inner choice we make, a choice we make every day, moment by moment.

All I see teaches me to trust the Creator for all I cannot see.

We have a part, a role, to play in a reality much larger than any we have dared to imagine or dreamed possible. We can never be deprived of our blessedness, but we can deprive ourselves of knowing it. If we argue for our limitations, we get to keep them. Struggle can become our identity if we empower our reasons and excuses rather than our divinity. Our life works when we have trust, vision, purpose, direction, action, joy and beauty.

We can't trust anyone else (including God), until we trust ourselves.

We have a responsibility to live in the exquisite wonder of it all, a state of expecting something worthy of celebration to occur in every moment.

Live a life of constant celebration
Live a life of wonder
Stop
Celebrate
Enjoy
Create beauty
As a natural expression of
Who and what you are
The limitless
Creative power of God
Is available
To each of us
We must be willing
To release false concepts of
Who we think we are
And to remember
We are unique
Unrepeatable miracles of God
We can let the past go
We can let the pain go
Only if we are willing
To have a new, free
Empowered life

We can see ourselves
As helpless
Imposed upon
Unappreciated
Or
Lovable
Capable
Appreciated
Powerful
There is nothing
The Power of God
Within us
Cannot do through us

Claiming our power is freedom. It allows us to have mastery over our lives. We are the energy of Divine expression. We have a responsibility to assert our authority as blessed beings.

Declare the truth of your being; claim your sacred heritage: "I AM God operating through my personality for the benefit of Earth, all species of life on the Earth and beyond. This is the truth of who I AM."

Ask to consciously become a "soul-infused personality." Recognize the power of your thoughts and the spoken words.

LAW OF MOVEMENT OR MOTION:

"An object at rest tends to remain at rest, and an object in motion tends to stay in motion, unless subject to an outside force." *Sir Isaac Newton*

LAW OF NEW BEGINNINGS:

For each of us, in our time, there are major life turning points. When there is a break in the energy wave patterns, a complete change will result. Everything is affected by this change in flux, some things to a lesser degree than others.

LAW OF NON-ATTACHMENT:

We are only temporary custodians, stewards of our possessions. What we own does not establish who we are. There is nothing wrong with having stuff; it is our attachment to it that leads us astray. When we are non-attached, we can surrender to the present moment and trust the Wisdom of the Universe will work in concert with our own inner wisdom to bring into our lives what is necessary for that moment to be blessed. When we attempt to control, we limit most of our possibilities for abundance and good. When we are in a possessive state of mind, be it possessive of things, ideas, or people, our energy is rigid, solidified, non-flowing, restrictive. That rigidity shows up as stuck energy in our body and consciousness, which results in stuck situations in our lives. In order for energy to work efficiently and effectively, it must be unrestricted, free-flowing.

LAW OF NON-INTERFERENCE:

To deliberately, or through ignorance, interfere in the life stream of another individual is to go against Universal Law. Unless we are asked by that person to intervene on their behalf, we have broken the Law. To decide what is best for another person and to pressure that person into following our will for their life is to break the Law.

Due to the *LAW OF NON-INTERFERENCE*, one species is not allowed to interfere in the progression of another species, without permission from within that species. This is the reason many extra-terrestrials have at this time agreed to come to Earth to be Humans and to remember who they really are and to give permission to the Spiritual Hierarchy, The Intergalactic Federation and the Angels to intervene in a positive way to promote the positive evolution of Earth, the Human species and all life on Earth.

One country, or a group of spiritual people, or politicians interfering in the life of another race, religion or political group is against spiritual Law, unless beings who are being oppressed or abused physically, mentally, emotionally or spiritually ask for their assistance or intervention.

We give our power away when we allow ourselves to become upset over another person or group's behavior, when we refuse to forgive and release hurt from the past. We give our power away when we keep a past wound festering in the present. When we believe we cannot live without another person, we give our power away. We imprison ourselves when we give our power away.

We are going against the *LAW OF NON-INTERFERENCE* when we pray for a specific outcome for another person against their will or desire. We are allowed to guide and "interfere" in the life of our children (the bodies we have created for other souls) during the time of our contract with the souls for which we created bodies. We are allowed to guide, to support and to be available to teach them. These contracts are different within each life stream of consciousness. We would be well advised to ask our souls for the details of each contract so as not to go beyond that contract and try to protect, depend upon, or arrange the life of another person and, thereby, interfere with their life lessons.

Each person who comes to Earth comes with a purpose, a destiny. It is our responsibility to promote our own self-development without retarding the progress or interfering with the well-being of another person or persons. It is not enough to refrain from intruding upon the affairs of others in deed only; we must abstain in thought, word and deed. When we allow ourselves to be consciously or unconsciously empathic, we intrude into the emotional body of another person. This is against the *LAW OF NON-INTERFERENCE*. We should never impose our way of thinking or living upon others.

LAW OF NON-JUDGMENT:

The Universal Spirit does not judge us; judgments are Human inventions, a means to compare, contrast and control. We judge ourselves against artificial, and often idealistic, standards of perfection, morality or truth. God did not invent morals; people did. Spirit never judges us, but gives us opportunities to balance and to learn. We are called not to judge others, but rather to discern what is correct for ourselves. There is a difference between judgment and discernment. When an individual discerns a situation energetically for him or her and makes a decision of behavior or involvement based on that discernment, this is not judgment.

Judgment involves telling another what is best for them or judging another's behavior as inappropriate for them. Judgment or gossip is to repeat our discernment of another person's behavior, looks or conscious-ness and then adding <u>this person will never change</u>. This addition changes discernment into judgment. Judgments block energy, set up internal defenses and resistance, and tend to hold negative patterns in place. We lock them energetically into our judgment of what is possible for them. Releasing judgment opens the way for change.

LAW OF NOURISHMENT:

The *LAW OF NOURISHMENT* governs the physical health of every Human being. Only natural food can properly nourish the Human body. Acid-forming foods build the body. Alkaline foods tear down, repair and eliminate the waste material from the body. To remain in optimum health, we are to eat a diet of three-fourths alkaline foods and one-fourth acidic foods. We are responsible for nourishing our minds, bodies and souls with positive thoughts.

LAW OF OBEDIENCE:

Our Higher Self knows us better than we know ourselves. If we listen to the voice of our intuition and then refuse to do the bidding of the soul, we are not fulfilling the *LAW OF OBEDIENCE*. Obedience to the soul's suggestions is one of our greatest tests. This does not mean, as I have stated before, we are not allowed to make conditions under which we can obey the suggestions of the soul.

LAW OF ONE:

Every soul, living and discarnate, is connected at the level of the collective unconscious, deep within the Higher Self. We are all part of a great energy gestalt called God, and because we are part of God, we are God. It is the goal of the gestalt to move the energy forward, creating more energy. So, in living harmoniously, we each increase our vibrational rate and intensify the vibration of the entire gestalt. When we are disharmonious, we decrease the vibration of the entire gestalt, because we are One; everything we think, say and do, affects every other soul.

LAW OF OPPOSITES:

We currently live in a Universe of duality. Each thing contains its opposite: Day/Night, Light/Dark, Tall/Short, Male/Female, and Up/Down.

LAW OF PARTICIPATION:

The soul makes suggestions through intuition. If we follow these suggestions, we fulfill the *LAW OF PARTICIPATION* and, therefore, qualify for the spiritual gifts that come from spiritual participation.

LAW OF PATIENCE:

Patience and faith are the two greatest tests of the Human soul. Practice surrender to the soul. We are given tests of patience – if we endure with patience, the events of divine timing will fall into place.

Patience is power; with time and patience, the mulberry leaf becomes silk.
CHINESE PROVERB

Everything has its season and every growing season requires the passage of a certain amount of time. This is our most challenging lesson as we live in a World of Humans motivated by instant gratification. Moving our consciousness out of our head, where we desire things to go our way now, and moving it into our hearts can help us move into the Universal flow of God.

LAW OF PATTERNS:

As children, we learn to make sense of the World by observing patterns. We experienced patterns of hunger and feeding, day and night, waking or sleeping, as we conformed to our parents' schedules and our own internal rhythms. By recognizing patterns in the noises our parents made, we learned the complex association of sound and meaning; through repeated patterns, we learned to speak. We grew to depend upon patterns repeating themselves, and we learned to repeat them – brushing our teeth and other nighttime rituals; patterns at home, at school and at work. By the time we were ten years old, the power of patterns had become part of our lives.

Any habit or pattern, whether we call it "good" or "bad," despite our best intentions, tends to reassert itself over time unless we break that pattern by doing something different.

This Universe is based on the mathematical progression of the pattern of the Golden Mean Curve. It is found inside the Nautilus shell, the end of the pineapple and in pinecones, etc. The Universe is held together by geometric patterns.

LAW OF PERFECTION:

The *LAW OF PERFECTION* presents a paradox because it contains two apparently opposite truths which operate at different levels of experience. From a transcendental perspective, everyone and everything is unconditionally perfect. From a conventional viewpoint, perfection does not exist. Excellence is the best we can achieve, and achieving it takes time, practice and patience.

All sorts of events, both beautiful and terrible, can happen in our World; some we like and approve of, while others we dislike and resist. Perfect faith recognizes that our mind cannot know or assume what is for our highest good; this faith inspires us to appreciate the perfection of seeming imperfection. Such recognition opens doors to an expanded sense of life. In terms of Human evolution, all is happening as it should.

LAW OF PERSONAL RETURN:

Although this Law is really just another way to view *THE LAW OF KARMA*, some people prefer it. It says if you think negatively of someone or send hateful thoughts to them, the thoughts may harm the person, but in due course, they will return to the sender as they were sent. The same is true of disharmonious deeds. But the good news is the *LAW OF PERSONAL RETURN* also works in reverse; the positive thoughts, words, and deeds will be returned to the sender.

LAW OF POWER:

THE LAW OF POWER comes from claiming the power of our divinity. We can claim our divinity and use this power to serve Humanity and the Earth which results in abundance in our lives. Using our minds, thoughts, will and physical strength to create results, rather than allowing the soul and Divine Will to work through us, causes pain, stress, anxiety and undesired karma in our lives and in the World.

LAW OF PRAISE:

Whatever we praise must turn into good. We have within us the power of praise, the power to bless.

LAW OF THE PRESENT MOMENT:

The idea of time is a convention of thought and language, a social agreement; in truth, we only have this moment. Time doesn't exist; what we refer to as "past" and "future" have no reality except in our own mental constructs. The *LAW OF THE PRESENT MOMENT* is not an abstract concept; time is the abstract concept. We almost never have a problem in the present moment. The *LAW OF THE PRESENT MOMENT* can sweep our psyche clear of debris and return us to a state of simplicity and inner peace.

LAW OF PROCESS:

On the path to our goals, if we desire to get from point A to point Z, the surest way to get there is to first go to point B, then C, then D, and so on. Skipping a single step, even though it appears to be a shortcut, often results in failure. We can break down any achievement or goal, no matter how large or imposing, into manageable steps. Every step becomes a small success in itself; that way, we succeed many times, not just when we reach our final goal. What we learn on the journey may turn out to be more important than reaching the destination.

LAW OF PROGRESSION:

If a soul has incurred and completed an incarnation without achieving a new level of growth, by not adding to its vibrations during the course of the incarnation, it must assume incarnation again almost immediately. All is always in a constant state of movement. If a soul is not constantly expanding its vibrations by exposing itself to new energies, its energies shall begin to dissipate. A soul may not remain stationary, for nothing is at rest. All is in a state of movement in a forward or dissipating vibratory spiral.

LAW OF PURIFYING ACTION:

We spiritually evolve by being generous, having moral restraint, not killing, not stealing, honesty, avoiding useless and frivolous talk and gossip, not committing sexual misconduct, not taking intoxicants which can clog the mind and make it dull. Meditation, concentration, eating healthy food, drinking water and the cultivation of insight, not only helps in our evolution, but also helps to purify our bodies.

LAW OF REALIZATION:

Realization is knowing, understanding and utilization, not just believing. To read something gives knowledge of something. This is not realization. Knowledge means absolutely nothing if it is not used. Realization is the flooding of the consciousness with a flash of understanding. Knowledge with usage becomes wisdom. Realization comes from self-awareness and other awareness.

LAW OF RECUPERATION:

Continuous, never-ceasing activity for any living thing means untimely death. To recuperate means to recover. With reference to the *LAW OF RECUPERATION*, it means to recover the energy one has expended during the day. There are three ways to recuperate: rest, recreation and sleep. Rest is the most important element in healthful living. Since Humans are creatures of reason, in order to remain healthy, one must have not only physical rest but also periods of cessation of all mental concentration.

LAW OF REFLECTION:

That which you admire in others, you recognize as existing in yourself. That which you resist in others, and react to strongly, is surely to be found within you. That which you resist, and react to in others, is something which you are afraid exists within you. That which you resist in yourself, you will dislike in others. We have chosen to incarnate, to rise above the effects of fear. Those fears will always be reflected in our reactions to others. As we let go of fear, we are automatically open to expressing more unconditional love.

LAW OF REINCARNATION:

Until we have resolved our karma and fulfilled our dharma, we will continue to reincarnate into sequential lifetimes upon the Earth or other planets. Neither God, nor the soul, nor the Lords of Karma bestow suffering upon us. We alone decide what we most need to learn and in our earthly sojourns we seek out other souls, often with shared histories, which can assist us to be confronted by these lessons. Once we balance our karma, we can decide to return to Earth or another planet to assist others.

LAW OF RELATIVITY:

Time and space are not separate entities, but are a smoothly linked part of a larger whole called the time-space continuum ($E=MC^2$). Everything in this Universe is a part of a continuum. Despite the apparent separateness of things at the physical level, everything is a seamless extension of everything else. We are all a part of something that has extended its uncountable energy into all the apparent objects, atoms, restless oceans and twinkling stars in the cosmos.

Matter does not exist independently from the sea we think of as empty space. It is a part of space. Space is not empty. It is the ground for the existence of everything, including ourselves.

Our almost universal tendency to fragment the World and ignore the dynamic interconnectedness of all things is responsible for many of our problems, not only in science, but in our lives and our society as well. For instance, we believe we can extract the valuable parts of the Earth without affecting the whole. We believe it is possible to treat parts of our body and not be concerned with the whole. We believe we can deal with various problems in our society, such as crime, poverty, and drug addiction, without addressing the problems in our society as a whole, and so on. Our current way of fragmenting the World into parts not only does not work, but may even lead to our extinction, but not the extinction of the World.

LAW OF RELEASE:

The *LAW OF RELEASE* involves letting go of anything that is no longer useful and purposeful, without regrets and without resentment. This includes such things as books, philosophy, clothing, belief, relationships, your lifestyle, organization memberships or religious affiliations.

LAW OF RESPONSIBILITY:

Working together, we can accomplish tasks that would be difficult or impossible without cooperative effort. Once we establish the limits and boundaries of our responsibility, we can take charge of that which is our duty and let go of that which is not; in doing so, we find more enjoyment supporting others as we create more harmonious cooperative relationships.

To become inappropriately responsible for another person to the extent we hinder them from being responsible for themselves, breaks the *LAW OF RESPONSIBILITY*. We enable them to remain weak or, in some cases, addicted to behaviors that go against the desires of their souls. We limit their spiritual growth by denying them the lessons of their behavior.

In our relationships with ourselves, with other people and with our own circumstances, we need to discover our point of balance; define and delineate the limits and boundaries of our appropriate level of responsibility; and to recognize our values, needs and priorities may rightfully be very different from those of our parents', siblings', spouse's, or other people's.

LAW OF RESTRICTION:

Humans cannot create anything higher than their level of energy and understanding. Society can never get any better than the level of Humankind as a whole. Our systems for social change usually only add new agencies, committees, or burdens to already ineffective systems. Time has proven this approach to a new society doesn't work, and our mistake is in trying to rectify the wrongs of the World from the outside in. This is working on the effect instead and is doomed to failure. Every one of us can incorporate the power of harmonious thinking which is the only long term solution to poverty and limitation. To heal the World we must each first heal ourselves.

LAW OF RITUAL:

Any act performed repeatedly with specific content and intention becomes a rite. Each time it is repeated, its power is enhanced in three ways. By focusing on the intent, the performer intensifies the power of their mind to control reality. The performer gives permission to their soul to assist them with the manifestation. Each performance of the rite draws upon the energy of all who have used the rite throughout all time.

LAW OF SANITATION:

Cleanliness is indispensable in keeping the body healthy, wholesome and beautiful. Not only does cleanliness affect the body, it also reaches to the confines of the mind, the soul and the Spirit. Since the body is the abode of the mind and the soul, and the instrument of the Spirit, these can evolve to higher planes of existence only in an environment that is clean, pure and orderly.

LAW OF SELF-DENIAL:

The person who judges themselves as unworthy shall be denied worthiness. Those who deem themselves as worthy will flow in the mainstream of prosperity. We have no right to deny the flow of the energy of God through us. It is not being humble to deny ourselves; it is being ignorant of who we truly are as conduits of God's energy. We should deny ourselves nothing that is offered to us which furthers our ability to accomplish our mission and have enjoyment of life.

LAW OF SELF-DESTRUCTION:

Unless we challenge ourselves we stagnate. We are energy and stagnation is self-destruction, for energy cannot stand still; it must, by its nature, move forward or backward. We are to always give ourselves new challenges. If we let the challenges be too great, self-destruction is the result. If we don't incorporate challenges into our lives, self-destruction is the result. We must keep challenge in balance to succeed in maintaining our position and retaining our success. The secret is to consciously direct challenge in a way that minimizes jeopardy while fulfilling balance.

LAW OF SELF-TRUTH:

Our truth is whatever we believe. If we believe something to be, it is truth for us even though it may not be a universal truth. Whatever we believe to be truth affects every area of our lives.

LAW OF SELF-WORTH:

We can only attract to ourselves things of which we feel worthy. Our self-esteem is critical to our happiness and success. We are not what we have and we are not what we do. Beneath our fear programming, we are perfect. It is only in our fear programming we keep ourselves from acknowledging who we really are as aspects of God. The more we can let go of fear, the higher our self-esteem will be and the more options we will have. The better we like ourselves, the better others will like us and the more worthy we will feel.

LAW OF THE SIXTH SENSE:

Intuition is the sixth sense, the capacity to know something without rational evidence that proves it to be so. The sixth sense is a subliminal sense Spirit endowed us with to maneuver safely through the maze that is real life. The sixth sense communicates with us in inventive ways; emotional trembling, goose bumps, hot or cold flashes, flashes of knowing, hunches, interior pictures, visions, dreams, voices or knowingness.

LAW OF SOCIO-METRIC INFLUENCE:

Matter coming into contact with other matter absorbs and influences as a result of the contact. A person wearing a piece of inherited jewelry, if they do not clear the previous wearer's vibrations, will be influenced by the vibrations of the previous wearer. The more empathic a person is, the more likely they will be influenced by the objects and people around them. As another example, when the contact takes place between two people, the intensity of the contact will dictate the degree and duration of the influence – so sexual union would result in a linked mental connection of the two people, even if they do not see each other again. Neither might recognize this consciously, but on an unconscious level, contact and energetic influence continues.

LAW OF SPIRITUAL UNION:

When a relationship between two souls has been established by blending and union of spiritual vibrations, the relationship will be blessed by the Oversouls and will perpetuate itself. When two people enter into a relationship based on conscious emotional involvement, whether it is sexual or expressed in another physical area, it shall be entered into because of the lessons involved between the two souls. If within this relationship, a spiritual relationship does not occur, the relationship shall dissipate and eventually end.

LAW OF SUMMARIZED EXPERIENCE:

We are the sum total of all that has ever happened to us in this life and in all our past lives. Everything from our health to our relationships, our sexual experiences, our developed abilities, our career standing and everything else, can be used as a scale to show who we are and to tell if our conscious and subconscious minds are functioning in harmony.

LAW OF SYMPATHY:

Sympathy often degenerates into a morbid sentimentalism that brings no stimulus to healthy effort and encouragement. Sympathy, used in the sense of sorrowing with others, is a violation of Natural Law and should not be indulged in. It is important to feel detached sympathy for individuals rather than empathy. To be sentimentally involved, sympathetically or empathically, brings the energy of the exchange to the lowest common denominator of feeling and does not bring the highest possible energy of healing to the situation. To hold the soul energy of charity, love and compassion (which is the energy of combined soul passion) with one who is suffering brings the energy of the soul into the situation and creates a positive possibility of healing.

When an individual no longer discriminates between races, creeds or color, when one's sympathetic consciousness encompasses all people in all stations of life – when one radiates a spirit of kindness, charity, patience and love to the whole body of Humankind – then the individual is expressing sympathy in its highest and most developed stage. Only through awareness of the ONENESS of Humankind can we acquire the quality of feeling that is characterized by mutual understanding and genuine helpfulness toward all people.

LAW OF TELEPATHY:

Telepathy is an impersonal universal principle. Vibrations make it possible for us to energetically communicate with each other mentally. As you are, so you will attract. Telepathy is active and present at whatever level of evolvement we have attained.

LAW OF THANKSGIVING:

Give thanks for all things great and small, "good" or "bad", for all things are for a purpose. Give thanks even for problems, for all problems there are solutions and in seeking the solutions we gain knowledge, which can lead us to wisdom.

LAW OF TOTALITY:

Each part of the totality has its own characteristic and also takes on the characteristics of the totality as a sum of its parts. Each part has two functions: to retain its own characteristics and to function as part of the totality. When separated, each part remains connected to the totality; and, because it retains the characteristics of the totality, it can perform as the totality. Now, you may not realize this yet, since you are part of God you contain the potential to perform as God. This LAW is often expressed as the *LAW OF ONE*.

LAW OF TRANSGRESSION:

Every transgression against your fellow Human must be righted or paid. Owe no person anything, whether it is a service, a kindness, money or a gift. If one does you a service or kindness, repay them by returning the service or kindness to another, any other; for in so doing, the first person is paid.

LAW OF VIBRATIONAL ATTAINMENT:

The entire Universe operates on the same principle of vibrational energy. When Einstein discovered matter is energy, he opened the door to merging science and metaphysics. The scientists have proven energy cannot die; it can only transform. By its very nature, energy must move backward or forward, it cannot stand still, for to do so is stagnation resulting in transformation. We are energy. Our skin, which appears solid, is actually trillions of swiftly moving molecules orbiting each other at a specific vibrational rate; a physical life rate we earned in the past as a result of how we have harmoniously or dis-harmoniously lived our past lives and our current life up until this very moment in time.

LAW OF VISION:

"Because you cannot see me with your own natural eye, I will give you a celestial eye."
- BHAGAVAD GITA

Often, what the physical eyes perceive is a very limited glimpse of reality. Sometimes it's a glimpse into the magnificent, but at other times it's a glimpse into the worst of Human conditions. Our physical eyes give us a limited view of reality. It is the awakening of our inner sight that can truly reveal reality to us. Until we awaken to the broader, gentler spiritual reality, we believe the picture our physical eyes send to us is the totality of possibilities, which is never true. Always ask to "know" the truth of any given situation.

"Other potential realities are right there before us veiled by the flimsiest of screens."
- William James

LAW OF WISDOM:

Knowledge without usage means nothing. Knowledge with understanding and usage becomes wisdom.

The Wisdom of God is hidden within the depths of every soul. We are now and forever one with the Divine. Having free will, we are capable of denying this great truth as our personal reality, but we maintain our ignorance by this denial. We are free to live in the misery of our own making, but we are not free to alter our true spiritual heritage. When we believe we are separate from God, we think He/She is separate from us and our lives reflect painful experiences of that false belief. We are capable of uniting with God Mind, joining in consciousness to create the kind of life we have only dreamed of. Here we begin to experience miracles, to trust the workings of a higher wisdom active in our lives. This wisdom is invaluable.

LAW OF THE WORD:

"In the beginning was the Word." Words create everything, because words are the embodiment of thought. Words come from fear or from faith and express our enthusiasm or our depression. Our words are the full transference of our energy from the psyche to physical expression. They are the magic wands of creativity. When we own our dream, own our words, we assume our true identity as a being made of Light in the image and likeness of the Creator. It is important to carefully and lovingly choose our words to specifically create the full intention of our dreams. We are to speak our words with focus, intention, commitment and love. Our word is Law. We are to speak without doubt. We are to never say what we don't want to experience; rather, to express our heart's desires. Divine Spirit in its infinite love has endowed us with the ability and the free will to create whatever we choose, good or bad. Creation begins with thoughts and proceeds to words, ends with manifestation, no matter if goals are good or bad, conscious or unconscious.

References

Universal Law for the Aquarian Age by Dr. Frank Alper

The Life You Were Born to Live by Alan Cohn from New World Library

A Course in Life by Joan Gatttuso from Jeremy P. Tarcher/Putnam

Your Heart's Desire by Sonia Choquette from Three Rivers Press

The Psyche and Psychism by Torkom Saraydarian from Aquarian Educational Group

Rays of Dawn by Thurman Fleet from Concept Therapy Institute

The Holographic Universe by Michael Talbot from Harper/Collins Publishers

Simple Abundance by Sarah Ban Breathnach from Warner Books

50 Primary Universal Laws by Dick Sutphen from Valley of the Sun

www.ingramcontent.com/pod-product-compliance
Lightning Source LLC
Chambersburg PA
CBHW021348090426
42742CB00008B/784